AROUND THE WORLD ON WHEELS
FOR THE INTER OCEAN

LECTOR HOUSE PUBLIC DOMAIN WORKS

AROUND THE WORLD ON WHEELS
FOR THE INTER OCEAN

H. DARWIN MCILRATH

ISBN: 978-93-90015-50-4

Published: 1898

© 2020
LECTOR HOUSE LLP

LECTOR HOUSE LLP
E-MAIL: lectorpublishing@gmail.com

AROUND THE WORLD ON WHEELS FOR THE INTER OCEAN

THE TRAVELS AND ADVENTURES IN FOREIGN LANDS —OF— MR. AND MRS. H. DARWIN MCILRATH.

BY

H. DARWIN MCILRATH

COMPILED FROM LETTERS WRITTEN BY MR. MCILRATH

AND PUBLISHED IN
THE SUNDAY AND WEEKLY INTER OCEAN,
FROM APRIL, 1895, TO NOVEMBER, 1898.

1898

THE TOUR AT A GLANCE.

CHAPTER XIV.

CHAPTER XV.

CHAPTER XVI.

CHAPTER XVII.

CHAPTER XVIII.

CHAPTER XIX.

CHAPTER XX.

CHAPTER XXI.

INTRODUCTORY.

PROPOSAL OF THE INTER OCEAN TOUR—ENTHUSIASTIC CHI-
CAGO WHEELMEN ATTEND THE RECEPTIONS TO THE CY-
CLISTS—THE START ON APRIL 10.

Beyond tests of speed involving championships and world's records, there have been few performances in the recent history of cycling to attract more general notice than the world's tour awheel of Mr. and Mrs. H. Darwin McIlrath. In the early Spring of 1895 the Chicago Inter Ocean, appreciating the great interest taken in cycling all over the country, planned this remarkable trip of more than 30,000 miles. From the moment of the first announcement of the McIlrath tour to the time of their home-coming, interest in and admiration for the Inter Ocean Cyclists never abated. Letters of inquiry at once began to come in so thick and fast to the Inter Ocean office, that to facilitate matters and more thoroughly acquaint the public with the details of the tour than could be done in the columns of the Inter Ocean, a series of receptions was tendered to the intrepid riders for several days prior to their start. The large room at 101 Madison Street, Chicago, was secured for the purpose, and for days Mr. and Mrs. McIlrath received their friends and admiring enthusiastic Chicago wheelmen. The crowds in front of the building became so great gradually that special policemen were detailed to keep the throng moving and traffic open. Among those who visited the McIlraths were:

Mrs. K. B. Cornell, President of the Ladies' Knickerbocker Cycling Club, Roy Keator of the Chicago Cycling Club, J. L. Stevens and W. C. Lewis of the Lincoln Cycling Club, Frank T. Fowler, Frank S. Donahue and Frank Bentson of the Illinois Cycling Club, O. H. V. Relihen of the Overland Cycling Club, Miss Annis Porter, holder of the Ladies' Century Record, Thomas Wolf, of Chicago-New York fame, Letter Carrier Smith, who has made the trip from New York to Chicago five times, David H. Dickinson, S. J. Wagner, O. Zimmerman (a cousin to the famous A. A.), Frank E. Borthman, R. B. Watson, Dr. and Mrs. W. S. Fowler, Mrs. J. Christian Baker, Mrs. L. Lawrence, John Palmer, President of Palmer Tire Co., Gus Steele, Yost racing team, C. Sterner and Grant P. Wright, Ashland Club, H. J. Jacobs, C. G. Sinsabaugh, editor of "Bearings," Mesdames A. G. Perry, George E. Baude, Helen Waters, D. W. Barr, C. Hogan, Mrs. Doctor Linden, George Pope, Robert Scott, Misses Kennedy, N. E. Hazard, Eva Christian, Mrs. Charles Harris, J. G. Cochrane, Pauline Wagner and Ada Bale.

Many of those who called, though utter strangers to the tourists, upon the strength of their friendship for the Inter Ocean brought letters of introduction for Mr. and Mrs. McIlrath to relations and acquaintances in the foreign lands to be visited. The itinerary as planned by the Inter Ocean was as follows:

Start from Chicago, April 10, 1895: Dixon, Ill.; Clinton, Cedar Rapids, Des Moines, Council Bluffs, Iowa; Omaha, Lincoln, Grand Island, Neb.; Denver, Pike's Peak, Colo.; Cheyenne, Laramie, Green River, Wyoming; Salt Lake City, Ogden, Utah; Elko, Reno, Nev.; Sacramento, San Francisco, Cal.; steamer to Yokohama, Kioto, Osaka, Niko, Kamachura, Papenburg, Japan; steamer to Hongkong and Canton, China; the Himalayas, Bangkok, Siam, Rangoon, Burmah; Calcutta, Benares, Lucknow, Cawnpore, Agro, Lahore, India; Jask, Teheran, Tabriz, Persia; Erzeroum, Constantinople, Turkey; Athens, Greece; steamer to Italy; Turento, Pompeii, Rome, Florence, Venice, Milan and Nice, Italy; Toulon, Marseilles, France; Barcelona, Valencia, Carthagena, Gibraltar, Spain; steamer across channel to Tangier and Cadiz; return via steamer to Gibraltar, Lisbon, Portugal; Madrid, Spain; Bordeaux, Orleans, Paris, France; Brussels, Belgium; Frankfort, Germany; Vienna, Austria; Berlin, Germany; Warsaw, Poland; St. Petersburg, Russia; steamer to Stockholm, Sweden; Christiana, Norway; steamer to Great Britain, Scotland, England and Ireland; steamer to New York, Buffalo, Erie, Penn.; Cleveland and Toledo, Ohio; Fort Wayne, Ind.; and Chicago.

It had been intended for the tourists to depart from Chicago at 7 o'clock on the morning of April 10. After farewell receptions at the Illinois Cycling Club and the Lake View Cycling Club, it was decided, in view of the popular demand, that the hour for departure be changed until noon. So it was that as the clock in the Inter Ocean tower struck 12 on Saturday, April 1, the credentials and passport, which was signed by Secretary of State Gresham, were given to Mr. McIlrath, and in the midst of a crowd numbering thousands, and with an escort of hundreds of Chicago wheelmen, the Inter Ocean cyclists were faced west and started on their tour of the globe.

Captain Byrnes of the Lake Front Police Station and a detail of police made a pathway through the crowd on Madison Street to Clark. Cable cars had been stopped and the windows of the tall buildings on each side of the street were filled with spectators. A great cheer went up as Mr. and Mrs. McIlrath mounted their wheels to proceed. They could go only a few yards so congested was the street, and they were forced to lead their wheels to Clark Street, north to Washington and west to Des Plaines. Here they mounted and the farewell procession was given its first opportunity to form. A carriage containing Frank T. Fowler, John F. Palmer, John M. Irwin and Lou M. Houseman, sporting editor of the Inter Ocean, led the way. Next came a barouche containing Mrs. Annie R. Boyer of Defiance, O., Mrs. McIlrath's mother. The escort of cyclers, four abreast, followed, with the tourists flanked by the secretaries of the Illinois and Lake View Cycling Clubs. At the Illinois Club House came the leave-taking, and not until then could the tourists be said to be fairly started.

The unlooked for events of the three years following 1895, chief among which was the Spanish-American War, caused several material changes in the itinerary of the McIlraths as originally planned. Though accomplished successfully, the long trip across Persia, taken during the dead of winter, resulted in delays that had not been anticipated and after the cyclists had entered Germany, it was deemed best by the promoters of the enterprise to bring the tour to an end. Mr. and Mrs. McIlrath left Southampton, England, the first week in October, 1898. After landing in New York they took a rest of several days before starting overland to Chicago. The route from New York to Chicago led through the following cities: New York to Yonkers, Poughkeepsie, Hudson, Albany, Schenectady, Canajoharie, Utica, Syracuse, Newark, Rochester, Buffalo, Fredonia, New York; Erie, Penn.; Geneva, Cleveland, Oberlin, Bellevue, Bowling Green, Napoleon, Bryan, Ohio; Butler, Kendallville, Goshen, South Bend, La Porte Ind.; through South Chicago and Englewood to the Inter Ocean Office.

[The McIlrath equipment consisted of truss-frame wheels made by Frank T. Fowler, of Chicago, fitted with Palmer tires and Christy saddles furnished by A. G. Spalding & Bro.]

CHAPTER I.

When I consented to the plan of going around the world I intended to make the trip alone, but my wife pleaded so hard to accompany me that I finally concluded to take her. She is a brave little girl, and rather than considering her a burden, I now look upon her as having been of great help to me on our memorable voyage. Aside from the fact that she is an expert wheelwoman, she is also an unerring shot. Nerve she possesses in abundance, as all will agree after reading of the adventures which befell us. The outfit with which we started did not exceed fifty pounds each. Both of us rode diamond truss-frame Fowler wheels, weighing 26 and 27 pounds each. The saddles were Christy anatomical, with Palmer tires, and everything from handle-bar to pedal was stoutly made. Mrs. McIlrath wore the "rational" costume so often derided by dress reformers, and I may say here, that had these same reformers witnessed the advantage of the "rational" costume upon some of the haps and mishaps which come to world's tourists, their arguments would be forever silenced. All of our luggage was carried in a leather case which neatly fitted the inside angles of the bicycle frames. Our personal apparel consisted merely of a change of underwear, as we depended upon the stores in towns along our route for new clothes whenever we should need them. The remainder of our luggage cases contained photograph films, medicines, repair outfits, etc. My "artillery," for which there was great use as it afterward happened, consisted of two 38-caliber and one 44-caliber revolvers.

To cyclists who contemplate a trip such as I have just made, or even one of lesser proportions, I can say that these three cannon are as necessary as a repair kit. They come in handy at the most unexpected times, and next to the pistols, I know of no better arms to carry than credentials from such a paper as the Inter Ocean. My credentials were necessary before we had been three hours out of Chicago, since through them we escaped an arrest, which meant certainly ten days or ten dollars. It happened in Melrose Park. We had come through Garfield Park to Washington Boulevard, through Austin, Oak Park and Melrose Park. The roads were abominable, and in order to take to the Northwestern tracks we were forced to return to Melrose Park. Being overjoyed at the sight of any smooth surface, we could not resist the temptation to ride on the sidewalks of this pretty suburb. Then it was that we were arrested. I pleaded with the officer and offered to pay a fine without the delay and inconvenience of standing trial, but he was firm in refusing to release us. At last I showed him my Inter Ocean credentials. Just as promptly he let us go, and remarking to a fellow officer that "it did not pay to buck against newspapers," he went so far as to assist Mrs. McIlrath on her wheel and start us again upon our way.

When we took the Northwestern tracks at Melrose Park our party numbered ten. They were: Ed. Porter, Tom Haywood, William Floyd, G. M. Williams, A. E. Wood, William J. Dilner, J. M. Bacon, F. W. Mechener, E. M. Lauterman and Miss Annis Porter. So far as Geneva, where we had supper, and where our escort left us to return to Chicago, the journey was without event. Two and a half days out from Chicago we were in Clinton, Iowa. We met friends all along the line who extended us hearty greetings. Not one of them was in ignorance of our tour and the Inter Ocean enterprise. Farmers called to us from their fields; engineers, as they whizzed by us, saluted with their whistles, and passengers in the coaches behind threw us notes, fruits and flowers. Since leaving Chicago we had eaten four meals daily, sandwiched with countless drafts of creamy milk, and yet the cry arose from us both, "I am so hungry." But the farmers were generous and we were never refused, and wherever remuneration was offered It was invariably declined.

We were met at Clinton by a party of twenty-five wheelmen and escorted into the city. Mrs. McIlrath and I had been reinforced by Messrs. William Boyd and J. E. Spofford of Dixon, Ill., through which city we had passed; Mrs. Scoville, who had been our hostess at Dixon, and herself so ardent a wheelwoman that she could not refrain from joining us for a few miles; and Harry Ferguson, a son of State Senator Ferguson of Sterling, Ill. When we left Clinton on Saturday, April 13, we had been invited by the press, municipal officers and the entire cycling fraternity to remain over for Sunday, which was Easter. The bright weather and the prospects of good roads, however, overweighed the social inducements, and we started at 4 o'clock Saturday afternoon. The promises of good weather were not fulfilled, and Mrs. McIlrath and I spent our Easter of '95 on the road in mud above our tires. In a chilling rain we rode into Cedar Rapids, where our entertainment and reception was royal. Frank Harold Putnam of the Merchants' National Bank, who, it is needless to say, is a devotee of the wheel, and his sister, Miss Caroline Putnam, of the Saturday Record, Cedar Rapids' society journal, gave us a warm greeting. With them we dined at the beautiful home of Mr. and Mrs. Charles Bell and through them we received from Messrs. C. D. Whelpley, Ben E. Miller and Harry Hodges of the Occidental Cycling Club, a letter of introduction to the Hon. Nicholas M. McIvor, United States Consul at Yokohama. There was much of interest to record during our stay in Cedar Rapids, chief of which was our visit to the Indian Reservation near Tama. Of this visit, I may mention that the squaws and the noble red men which came under our observation were more than sufficient to disillusion us, who had been fond readers of Longfellow's "Hiawatha."

MR. AND MRS. H. DARWIN McILRATH.

[From photographs taken two years ago in China.]

Hard riding, rain and the consequent exposure had got in its work upon me by the time we struck Marshalltown, but on the 19th, in spite of the advice of physicians, I started our party, being aided in the carrying of luggage by Mr. Ferguson, who remained with us. At 4:30 o'clock on the afternoon of April 19 we pedaled into Des Moines, the capital of Iowa. The dime museum man was on the alert for us, and we had been in the Kirk wood Hotel scarcely half an hour before my wife and I were offered $25 an hour each, for four hours' exhibition of ourselves. It is a waste of ink to say that the offer was declined without thanks. Our night in Des Moines was the most comfortable we had yet spent. The following day we were entertained at the State House by Governor and Mrs. Jackson and Private Secretary Richards. The Governor is a hearty believer in better roads and he is an admirer of cycling. He expressed sincere admiration for the world's tour awheel, and declared his admiration for the Inter Ocean in furthering such a project. The Des Moines Wheel Club entertained us lavishly in the evening, though while at the club house the tour of the globe was menaced with sudden termination. The brand of Marshalltown fever, which I carried away with me, was such that a physician ordered me promptly to bed. The sun, I am confident, was responsible for my condition. We had been out of Chicago ten days, and two-thirds of the distance was done over railroad beds. We had journeyed almost 300 miles over ties and trestles, suffering intermittently with paralysis of the hands. Often we were compelled to ride along a narrow shelf scarcely 12 inches in width just outside the track and ballast, where the slightest deviation from the course would have caused a plunge down an embankment frequently 30 feet deep. This, too, was accomplished upon a heavy laden wheel with the glare of the burnished steel in our eyes. My physician's advice was that I remain for several days in Des Moines, but anxiety to reach the coast moved me to depart Sunday, April 21. Fifty cyclists rode out of town with us and saw us fairly upon our hilly ride to Council Bluffs. Bad weather was encountered, delaying our arrival in Council Bluffs until April 23. Wheelmen from Omaha and Council Bluffs awaited us upon the outskirts of the latter named city, and in triumph we rolled into that splendid center of the Republic—Omaha. Here we found that the veteran Jack Prince had stirred much enthusiasm in wheeling, and a banquet at the "Pump House" was the first of the chain of entertainment in store. The "Pump House," it should be known, is a handsomely appointed club house under the patronage of the Omaha Wheel Club. Its name is derived from a large pneumatic pump which stands invitingly to all cyclists outside of the main entrance. Our stay in Omaha was pleasant and, from our selfish standpoint, only too brief. When we started away the afternoon of April 25, a pretty surprise and compliment was Mrs. McIlrath's when she found her wheel literally one of gorgeous flowers. Since we left Chicago no larger crowd has wished us good-bye than the one in Omaha. Our friend Ferguson left us here, stubbornly refusing to bear back with him our cargo of souvenir spoons. These precious mementos are all very well in their way, but hardly the thing for two persons who intend pedaling their way over the world. We were already threatened with having to charge ourselves excess baggage. Lincoln, the capital of the state, turned out almost to a man to receive us. The Capital City Cycling Club escorted us on our visit to Governor Holcomb, to whom we presented a letter of introduction. It was through the kindness of the Governor that we visited the State University, and with him we attended the theater in the evening.

CHAPTER II.

CYCLING IN A HAIL-STORM—A MEETING WITH A ONE-LEGGED WHEELMAN—"TOMMY ATKINS" JOINS THE PARTY—MT. ROSA'S BLIZZARD.

Grand Island, Neb., is a small city, but it contains more wheelmen, in proportion to its size, than any city we encountered. There are two bicyclists' clubs, the "Tourists" and "Orientals," the former an organization composed exclusively of ladies. Splendid delegations from both bodies were awaiting us outside of Grand Island the morning we neared the city. En route, Mrs. McIlrath experienced an accident which made me fear for her safety of limb, as well as fearing that we should be delayed for several days. About ten miles east of Grand Island, while riding the railroad tracks, we ran into a hail-storm. Mrs. McIlrath, with her head between her shoulders, was driving blindly in the face of the fusillade of ice bullets. Unable to see where she was going, she ran straight into a cattle guard, throwing her some twenty feet down an embankment, and bending her handle-bars till they met above. Our stay at Grand Island was limited, and we proceeded the same afternoon to Kearney, at which city we arrived late the following morning. Our party, which was much like a snowball, in that it gathered constantly, was augmented at Kearney by Mr. W. B. Walker. The trip was an eventful one for him, and probably changed his views upon the matter of wheelmen's costume. Walker was a howling swell when he started away with us. His Scotch clothes were models of the tailor's art, his cap was of the latest fashion, and his stockings were positively delirious in their pattern. At Shelby we struck an electrical storm, the lightning fairly gliding along the rails and ofttimes playing about our plated handle-bars. Walker grew frightened, and leaping from his wheel landed squarely in a pool of water, which had been stagnant until stirred by the heavy rain shortly before. He was anything but the dapper looking individual of Kearney when he dragged himself from the pool. He got as far as Cozad, and in tones of disgust he bade us good-bye to return home to his wardrobe.

We passed the night at Cozad, leaving there at noon Tuesday. At Gothenburg we were met by Will Edwards, S. P. Anderson and George Roberts. This man Roberts is a marvel. Some years ago he had the misfortune to lose his right leg, but put him on a wheel and he is a wonder in spite of his affliction. Through the sandy soil and mud, this man could even outwind Mrs. McIlrath and myself, and a picturesque figure he was, too, as he glided over the plains, with his one leg turning the pedal like a steam piston, and a crutch lashed over his back like a musket. The boys rode with us to North Platt, where we put up for the night. North Platt is one of the best known cities in Nebraska, made so, no doubt, by its being the home of

Col. W. F. Cody, famed all over the world as "Buffalo Bill." Cody has a magnificent ranch, which is virtually a present from the United States Government, as Uncle Sam donated the land in recognition of the Colonel's valuable services as scout during the Indian wars. The ranch is called "Scout's Rest," and is managed by Mr. J. A. Goodman, Col. Cody's brother-in-law. Our party spent a delightful day at the "Rest" and in the evening we were driven to the city residence of Col. and Mrs. Cody.

We landed upon Colorado soil on Friday, May 3, being accompanied from Big Springs, our last stop in Nebraska, by Messrs. Weber and Hoagland. I may mention, by the way, that Big Springs first achieved notoriety as the headquarters for the James gang. There are men still in Big Springs who delight to sit by the hour and relate their personal experiences with the daring Jesse and Frank, and their fearless followers. As we landed at Julesburg, our first stop in Colorado, on May 3, we made the 1,000-mile mark, the actual traveling time being fourteen days, which I did not consider bad in view of our traveling impedimenta and unfamiliarity with the roads. The roughest traveling we had yet suffered came between Red Line and Iliff. Along the line we found the natives to be the same kind-hearted, simple folk that cheered us on our way through Iowa and Nebraska. As an instance of the good-natured but gruff treatment we received, I cannot refrain from relating an experience at a section-house near Stoneham. Mrs. McIlrath was thirsty. For nearly six hours we had ridden in the blazing sun without catching so much as a sight of water. Our joy at beholding some evidence of human habitation proved almost too much for her. As we neared the section-house the little woman was all but in tears, and so impatient that she could hardly make the distance. We called at every window and door of the house, but not a soul replied. I peered into one of the little windows, and saw a bucket and dipper on a table. Thinking it no harm to enter without the owner's permission, I tried the front door, and to my bitter disappointment I discovered it locked with a big red padlock, bigger and redder than those the sheriff uses when he closes up a man's business house. Mrs. McIlrath was seated on the ground with tears rolling down her cheeks. The sight of her distress was more than I could bear. I was on the point of attempting to break the windows when I saw the tiny prints made by the wheels of a baby buggy rolling around the house. I knew at once that the family could not be far away, so leaving my wife with a promise to return shortly, I followed the tracks of the baby buggy and came upon the entire family in a pasture about a quarter of a mile from the dwelling. The section foreman greeted me in friendly tones, and asked what he could do. I told him it was water I wanted, and then as a guarantee of my honest intentions, I jokingly told him of my temptation to break his window.

"Young man," he replied sternly, "you are a fool. If my wife had been thirsty, and I could have found an ax, I shouldn't have walked this far to ask for a drink of water."

To appreciate thirst, or rather the cause for it, in this part of the country, it must be understood that all water is brought to the section-houses in barrels by the railroad company. Not a drop is wasted, the casks are watched and guarded as rigidly as the fresh water casks on a steamer at sea. Only once on our trip were we refused a bite to eat; food was always given us willingly and lavishly, but in many places it was like pulling teeth to get a cup of cold water from some of the inhabitants. On May 6 we covered 128 miles, riding over cactus, prairie and sandy desert. In the afternoon we arrived in Denver, marking our 1,200 miles out of Chicago, 500 of which had been done over railroad ties. Our comfort and entertainment in Denver were looked after by the "Ramblers." They were so kind to us that I feared we would be handicapped. I mean this literally, for each member seemed to think that he, solely, was paying Mrs. McIlrath the compliment of a souvenir spoon. It seemed impossible for us to get away from souvenir spoons. We had many pounds of souvenir spoons after a reception on the evening of May 8, at the Rambler's Club House. Poor Mrs. McIlrath wilted when we reached the hotel, and with a look of pleading that was comical to behold, she sank upon the bed and exclaimed:

"Oh, Darwin, how on earth are we ever to get around the world if we keep on adding weight to our clothes and traveling cases!" The reception at the "Ramblers" was a delightful event, and one which Mrs. McIlrath and I often talked of during our travels. We said good-bye to Denver at 3 o'clock on the afternoon of May 10. An escort of "Ramblers" followed us as far as Colorado Springs, upon the outskirts of which city we found awaiting us Messrs. C. W. Dawson, local consul for the L. A. W., A. C. Van Cott and L. J. Wahl. It was at Colorado Springs also that we met "Tommy Atkins," who was destined to be our steady companion. "Tommy Atkins" is the name which we gave to Merton Duxbury, an Englishman, who had left Providence, R. I., two weeks before we left Chicago. He was bound for 'Frisco, and by hard riding had arrived in Colorado Springs but an hour or two ahead of the Inter Ocean tourists. I do not know what we should have done without Duxbury. He was original in all things, a born comedian, in fact, though he himself did not know how delightfully amusing he was. If Mrs. McIlrath was tired, or hungry, or thirsty, and I wished to make her forget it, I had only to call "Tommy Atkins," and his pranks did the rest. More amusing things happened to "Tommy" than one could find by attending the theater nightly for years. Another "joy" in human form joined us at Manitou, in the person of "Jim" P. Anderson of Denver, a 200-pound cyclist who was trying to make himself thin by means of the wheel. He asked permission, which was readily given, to become one of us for a short time. With all regard for Anderson's staying qualities, I am inclined to believe it was just as well he did not ask to remain a longer time. But for the largest bottle in our medicine kit, he would have collapsed on our first hard ride up Cheyenne Mountain to Cripple Creek. A storm of blended rain, snow and sand had befallen us on our eight-mile climb to the peak of Mount Rosa, and at its thickest the gigantic Anderson dismounted from his wheel, and upon his knees in a snowdrift he offered a prayer to "dear, good, kind Mr. McIlrath" not to try to go farther, but to set back for the tavern at the base of the mountain. Upon this point I was immovable. The snow blinded the way ahead of us, but I insisted that we push on. After a few hundred yards my eyes were delighted with a sign reading, "Halfway House, Mount Rosa," and a wooden hand pointing up the mountain.

Pushing our snow-clogged wheels over an unbroken track we came to a log hut just back of the welcome sign, and there we discovered not a haven of rest and warmth, but a deserted house with its every door and window nailed. Poor Jim, with a hoarse cry, threw himself on the snow, and moaned like a child. Had we been lost in a desert, thousands of miles from aid, the situation could not have been more dramatic. Electricity now added its terrors to our discomforts, and with a sharp crackling sound everything assumed a pinkish hue. Contact with each other produced distinct shocks, and if our fingers touched the wire fence, against which we had leaned our wheels, tiny sparks darted from their tips to the attractive metal. It was only the grandeur of the scene, I firmly believe, that kept Mrs. McIlrath upon her feet. With Anderson it was no joke. The poor fellow was worn out, and the altitude had an effect upon his lungs that threatened him with severe hemorrhage. But "Tommy Atkins" stood the test nobly, and while he reassured Mrs. McIlrath, I did my best to brace up the inconsolable Anderson. Duxbury and I were agreed that as long as the sign directing us to the Halfway House remained standing there must be a Halfway House somewhere not far up the road. Anderson pulled himself together, and the four of us, pushing our wheels in single file, found the Halfway House one mile away. No palace was ever more attractive to the eye than was this house of plank, with its uncarpeted floors and unvarnished doors. The best meal we ever had was had in this hut. We passed the night here, and as we sat about the dining-room before going to bed, we made the acquaintance of Mr. George Bentley, an attorney of Colorado Springs, who was en route to Cripple Creek in a buggy. The meeting with Bentley was most fortunate for Anderson. The big wheelman lost no time in getting chummy with the lawyer, and as we started to retire Anderson surprised us all by exclaiming in the most matter-of-fact way: "Well, I thank you Mr. Bentley, and since you have suggested it, I shall be glad to ride to Cripple Creek in your buggy with you to-morrow." The cunning fellow had got ahead of us, and he thought it a great joke. With his wheel tied behind the buggy, he and Bentley left for Cripple Creek at 8:30 o'clock the next morning, and an hour afterward Mrs. McIlrath, "Tommy Atkins" and I followed in their wake.

We had been on the road an hour when, from a man we met on the crest of one of the hills just east of Love Camp, we learned that the buggy was not fifteen minutes ahead. With renewed vigor we set out to make up the time down that and every succeeding hill. The first hill was descended in safety and without effort we rolled up the short incline and plunged down the next. As I whizzed along, my wheel bending from side to side, I felt the road unusually rough and made strenuous efforts to slacken my speed. Duxbury was just ahead of me and I dared not remove my feet from the pedals for fear of running him down. Nor could I check my wheel too much, or Mrs. McIlrath would telescope me from behind. The situation was a trying one, and only when the last curve was reached, and I had successfully scraped past a large boulder which obstructed a clear passage over a corduroy bridge, did I feel safe. The place I had just passed was a most dangerous one. The bridge was narrow and the gorge was ten or twelve feet deep, and more than half filled with rushing water from the thawing snow. I was just wondering what would save one from death if a ride such as mine should terminate in striking a boulder in the path, when down the hill rushed my wife. The front wheel of her machine struck the rock, and with a scream the little woman was thrown foremost on the stones below, and disappeared under the foaming flood. Horror stricken, for a moment I stood spellbound, and then rushed forward expecting to find her terribly mangled, if not killed outright. When I reached the stream she was clinging to a crag, half the time completely submerged, her wheel about her neck like a frame. Fortunately she was unhurt beyond a few scratches and a bruise on the left cheek. Strangling and coughing she clung to the rock until I lifted the bicycle from about her and then Duxbury and I by much effort raised the brave woman to the bank above. Her wheel was uninjured, and after we had squeezed some of the water from her clothes, we ascended the "Divide" and pushed on until we came to a hut bearing a sign, "CRPL KRK Laundry." A Chinaman stood in the doorway, and from him we learned that Cripple Creek was just over the hill. When we reached the town "Tommy Atkins" escorted Mrs. McIlrath to our hotel, while I went to the postoffice for mail.

CHAPTER III.

Among my letters was one bearing a check from the Inter Ocean, and I lost no time in going to the bank to obtain the money upon it. The cashier required strong identification, which I, being a stranger, was of course unable to give. I then applied to President Lindsay in person. Mr. Lindsay, I am proud to record, is a gentleman who reads the newspapers. He had already heard of the Inter Ocean cyclists, and when he saw me he said: "My friend, you appear honest, and you look all you say you are, when it comes to riding across the country. It is a compliment when I tell you that you almost look like a tramp. Go get your money," and he nodded to the cashier. At the hotel I found everybody well and eating, "Jim" P. Anderson doing some especially good work with a knife and fork. Mrs. McIlrath had dried her clothes and was none the worse for her icy bath. Cripple Creek by gaslight is quite an attractive place for a "rounder," as I learned that evening, when with guides the gentlemen of our party visited the dance halls, colored people's "rags" and free-and-easy theaters that line "Push Street." The next day was spent in a visit to the El Paso and other mines. Friday, May 28, was scheduled for our departure, but rain made it impossible. Saturday, however, we got away at 6:30 in the morning for Leadville by way of Florrisant, Hartzel, Buena Vista and Granite. We had a day of hard riding, and by 8 o'clock in the evening Mrs. McIlrath was ill and too fagged to go further. After supper at the house of a road overseer, we came to a ranch, where we applied for shelter. For the first time since we had left Chicago we were bluntly refused. Mrs. McIlrath cried aloud when a gray-bearded, hook-nosed old man told her that he had no place for her to sleep. I argued to him that she was ill, but he shut off my pleading by telling me that two miles away was a hotel that had been built expressly for the accommodation of invalids. There was nothing to do but trudge on to this hotel, which we found to be the Hartzel Springs House, owned by and named for the gray-bearded gentleman who had without courtesy closed his doors in our face.

We started Sunday morning on a 60-mile run to Buena Vista, following the railroad tracks. At Hill Top we unexpectedly met Editor-in-Chief Martin of the Rocky Mountain News, and several other writers from the Denver papers. They fell in line with us, but wished to take their time in admiring the beautiful scenery; but upon Duxbury's suggestion that we "could not eat the blooming scenery," they relented and we pushed on to Buena Vista, where we arrived on the 26th. Here we were entertained by Ed. Krueger, now a cyclist of national fame, Mr.

and Mrs. Dean and Mr. and Mrs. C. Jones. The following day we went out to Hot Springs to see Krueger attempt to break the world's five-mile coasting record. After dinner at the Hot Springs hotel we began preparations for Krueger's race. The wind had subsided as if especially for his benefit. He was not satisfied with his own machine, believing it not strong enough for the test, so he used my wheel with his own saddle, handle-bars and pedals. Dean, Jones and Mr. Mason and myself acted as timers, and Duxbury officiated as starter. At 4 o'clock Krueger mounted his wheel and shot down the hill. Duxbury had taken the time of his start, and it was left for us to note the moment of his arrival. By subtracting the difference, and also splitting the variation of time in the watches of the four timers at the end of the course, we were enabled to gain a fairly accurate estimate of the traveling time. Krueger lost both pedals half way down the incline, but he curled his feet up and crossed the line in 10 minutes and 10 seconds, which I consider wonderful. We started the next morning, May 28, for Leadville, with Krueger also in the party. It was my turn for a disaster, and I came near bringing the Inter Ocean tour to a finish. In crossing a bridge of pine logs my front wheel slipped, and with one foot entangled in the spokes of the rear wheel I stood, eyes protruding, staring at a black rock 300 feet below. A move backward with one foot on terra firma might prove fatal, and to attempt to disengage the other foot meant the release and loss of the bicycle. Nothing remained but to fall backwards on the hard road in a sitting posture, which I did, and Mrs. McIlrath rescued me, scolding as a mother would a disobedient child. We made but a short day of it in Leadville for various reasons, principally that Duxbury was seized with the hemorrhage which threatened him on Mount Rosa. At 5 in the afternoon we left for Red Cliffe, 35 miles away. At the mouth of the Tennessee Pass Tunnel, eleven miles from Leadville, we were overtaken by another storm, more violent than any we had yet passed through. We were made prisoners in the tunnel for an hour or more, the dense blackness rendering it impossible for us to proceed with any degree of safety. Cautiously feeling our way along the walls we managed to emerge from the tunnel and in the night to pedal along to the nearest section-house. This turned out to be a disused box car with bunks built along the sides for the section hands. The section boss, a kind-hearted Irishman, readily gave us permission to stretch ourselves on the floor for a night's rest. We were soon asleep, but about 11 o'clock he waked us and informed us that he was sorry, but he could not help being forced to ask us to leave. The reason, he explained, was that his wife had suddenly returned and that she was the real "boss" of the establishment. As she had not been consulted in the beginning upon the matter of having us for lodgers she had declined to let us remain as her husband's guests. I begged and implored but without avail, and in a storm we set off for the telegraph office, half a mile away. The operator was a young woman and the sight of one of her sisters in distress was more than enough to win an invitation to make ourselves as comfortable as the office would allow. I was enraged almost to the point of personal violence at the thought of an ill-tempered woman's whim causing us such needless annoyance, but as it afterward transpired our experience with the woman section boss was but trivial. It is an even break in this part of the country what manner of treatment a touring wheelman will receive at the hands of the people.

A pleasant surprise was ours the morning we rode into Glenwood Springs, Colo., and registered at the palatial Colorado Hotel. A party of Chicagoans, composed of Mr. and Mrs. W. J. Hynes, Mrs. Hynes' mother and sister, Mrs. and Miss Way, en route from California, were at the hotel and soon made themselves known. They had been present at one of the Inter Ocean receptions to us in Chicago and the pleasure of meeting was therefore doubled. We spent the night at Glenwood Springs, leaving the morning of May 31. An accident to Mrs. McIlrath on June 2 between Palisades and DuBeque delayed us the greater part of the week. It was the machine that suffered the real damage, although she herself was rendered unconscious for half an hour. In riding over a sluice she took a tumble, but the accident was not discovered for some moments afterward. I chanced to look over my shoulder and saw her figure stretched in the middle of the road with the machine a shapeless mass by her side. "Tommy Atkins" and I worked hard to revive her, and the walk to DuBeque, six miles ahead, was one of the greatest efforts she was called on to put forth during our entire journey. There was no repair shop in DuBeque, and it was evident at once that we should have to take a freight train for Grand Junction, the nearest point at which we might expect repairs. Our stay at Grand Junction was pleasant in the extreme, and we certainly did not begrudge the three days spent in the city waiting the repairs to arrive from Chicago. Friends who had heard of our tour met us at Grand Junction and straightway began exerting themselves for our entertainment. Their program embraced a visit to Teller Institute, an Indian school near by, and on the evening of our second day a complimentary dinner was given the Inter Ocean tourists by Judge Gray, a jolly, 300-pound enthusiast upon all topics pertaining to the wheel. On June 8 the fork for Mrs. McIlrath's wheel arrived from Chicago, and an hour later we were ready for one of the most difficult stages of our entire trip, that of crossing 290 miles of desert between Grand Junction and Springville, Utah. Tom Roe, known to every cyclist from coast to coast, once attempted it on his ride from San Francisco to New York City and failed. John McGuire, editor of the Cycling West, who has wheeled from Denver to Salt Lake City three times, never succeeded in crossing the desert entirely. When we announced that it was our intention to make it without a break from boundary to boundary, there was a general laugh of ridicule on all sides. Every one predicted that we would fail before we had done 100 miles from Grand Junction. We left at noon and rolled out on the white sandy roads, making 12 miles before the first stop. The great difficulties of our trip across the desert proved to be not so much the hard ploughing through sand as the general inhospitality characteristic of the section houses which dot the vast waste. The section hands are mostly Italians and Chinamen, with a fair sprinkling of Indians. Asked for food or water, they either would not or pretended they could not understand. As the next town from Fruita, our first stop, was 67 miles distant, it will be guessed that we had many a trying meeting with section hands before we came to a hotel. We had been led to expect no kindness from these foreigners, but "Tommy Atkins" and I had sworn to win to our side every man that chance placed in our way. Some of our efforts to make ourselves agreeable in hopes of a hearty welcome were ludicrous.

At a ranch near Westwater our party was refused shelter, the mother of three sons residing there telling us that the boys were away from home, one of them having gone to the next settlement for provisions. The pantry, she said, was all but empty, and were she to take in three hungry persons like myself, Mrs. McIlrath and Duxbury, there would be nothing left by the next morning. It was an uncertainty when the supplies were to arrive and a former experience had made her firm in her intentions to take no risks when food promised to be scarce. Our combined entreaties weakened the old lady to the extent that she consented to take in Mrs. McIlrath at least. She warned us that Mrs. McIlrath would have nothing to eat but bread and milk, but then even bread and milk seemed more than a dinner at Chicago's best hotel, and leaving my wife with her benefactress, Duxbury and I went forth determined to charm the Italians at the section house we had passed a few miles back. As soon as we had convinced the Italians that we were not in the service of the railroad as private detectives, or that we were not a pair of the thousands of tramps making the journey from coast to coast on foot, they not only gave us supper but volunteered permission to spend the night before their fire. When we started the next morning I offered money to the section boss, but he declined it, saying I could repay him by delivering a letter which he handed me, addressed to his brother at a section house a few hundred miles ahead.

As I have remarked before, the scarcity of water in this part of the country necessitates the shipment of it to the section houses and stations by the railroads. This same scarcity of water was indirectly responsible for a serious accident to my bicycle. I mention it here to show wheelmen what can be accomplished in the way of impromptu repairing when the emergency demands it. The tramps who steal rides on the freight trains never go without a bottle or a tin can of water. As these vessels are drained of their precious contents at different intervals along the roadbed, "Weary Willie" is in the habit of throwing them away. The result is that the tracks for miles and miles are spangled with bits of sharp glass and tin. I was not aware of the risk I was taking with my tire until I ran over one of these "mines." There was an explosion like a shotgun, and when I found myself on the ground I realized that it was not the "mine" that had exploded, but my pneumatic. The puncture was, properly speaking, a gash three inches long in the tire of my rear wheel. Here was a pretty state of affairs! Not a dealer in supplies or a repair shop within 100 miles, and not one of the party with a complete repair kit. There seemed no alternative but a long walk to the nearest section house or ranch, there to await until "Tommy Atkins" could make the next town and express me the needed material. But "necessity is the mother of invention," and under the press of circumstances I hit upon a scheme which afterward proved to work like a charm. First, I wet the edges of the rent with cement, sewing them together superficially, or, as the ladies would say, I "basted" them. Then I made a covering out of pieces of a buckskin glove, moistened with medicines from one of my vials. This covering I stretched on as tightly as possible over the gap. Now came a coat of cement, then the tire tape covering all, and my repair was as complete as I could make it until a cycle supply house could be found or my advance luggage reached. I did not jump on my wheel and ride directly, realizing that until the buckskin had dried and shrunken nothing was to hold the parted ends of tire but a few slight stitches. Mrs. McIlrath then came forward with a suggestion which was acted upon and proving itself to be one of much wisdom. It was that she take my mended tire and place it on her front wheel, where the pressure would be slightest, putting her front tire upon the rear wheel of my machine. For the benefit of doubting wheelmen, I must add that with three inflations daily, the crude mend held itself and answered purposes until Salt Lake City was reached a week later.

CHAPTER IV.

Utah I found to be full of snakes, lizards and swollen streams. Mrs. McIlrath, Duxbury and I had personal encounters in this direction and our escapes were thrilling. It was on our way to Thistle Junction Gap that Duxbury sprinted ahead, promising to meet us at the next railroad crossing. How he came to wind up on the side of a foaming torrent is beyond me to explain. I know only that when we came to the appointed meeting place, my wife and I stood upon one side of a miniature river with the hapless "Tommy Atkins" on the other bank. He was in a bad fix, for he could not swim—bye the bye, a most uncommon thing among Englishmen. He called for aid and without thinking that the man would be so rash as to follow my instructions, I told him to wade across. He thereupon walked into the water and there came very nearly being some work for the coroner. With his wheel held high above his head he walked boldly into midstream until he came to a step-off. I called to him to be cautious and not to move from where he was. With the warning I walked from the opposite bank ready at any moment to strike out with swimming strokes, but I ascertained that though the current was rapid, the water was no deeper than where Duxbury stood submerged to his shoulders. Lifting the wheel I led the way back to the bank, where "Tommy" stretched himself in the sun to dry. Had the boy not possessed nerve and retained his presence of mind I fear we should have seen the last of him when he made his unlooked-for descent.

Continuing our journey through Jordan Valley, Mrs. McIlrath rode some distance ahead of us. We were startled by shrieks, and it was my first thought that she had ridden over a snake. Duxbury and I hastened to her and discovered her standing by her wheel with a number of lizards gliding their way through the grass and sand at her feet. To show her that the silent crawlers were not poisonous, I picked one up in my hand, and was making bold with the ugly thing when a sharp rattle attracted my attention. Looking to one side, but a few paces away, I saw a five-foot rattler coiled as if to strike, and moving his fangs threateningly. My 44-caliber revolver settled Mr. Snake and the encounter also came near settling Mrs. McIl-rath. She was so nervous from the shock that it was with difficulty we proceeded to Springville. By a mistake of the telegraph operator we missed the Springville reception committee, and proceeded straight on to Provo City, where we spent the night. The next day Mayor Holbrook, James Clave, editor of the Inquirer, Robert Skelton and a dozen of the Provo City wheelmen called upon us and offered us the keys of the town. They invited us to spend several days with them, mapping out a program of lavish entertainment. This we were forced to decline, as we were impatient to get into Salt Lake City for bicycle repairs and sundry changes in our much dilapidated toilet. We arrived in Salt Lake City the morning of June 15, under the guidance of the Social Wheel Club. Sunday, the club members took us on a "Strawberry Run" to Farmington, though the acceptance of this invitation necessitated declining one to attend the run of the Wasatch Wheelmen. In the evening with Mr. Goode, Mr. Lenne of Chicago, Duxbury and myself went out to Saltair, the great resort a few miles from the city. On June 19 we were guests of the Beck Hot Springs Bicycle Club, where we watched the "crackerjacks" of Salt Lake City and Ogden. This track is one of the best I have seen upon my travels. "Big Bill" Richel, editor of the Rocky Mountain Cyclist, a man who has done much good work in building up interests in wheeling throughout the West, is a prime factor in the racing meets at Beck Hot Springs, and he has invariably arranged for a first-class article of sport. Our entertainment in Salt Lake City was upon so extensive a scale that I had no more than enough time to prepare my Inter Ocean letters and to send our wheels to the repair shop.

We left Salt Lake City on June 23, an escort of thirty accompanying us West as far as the Grant Homestead, where a stop was made for dinner. We arrived in Ogden the following day, expecting to leave in the evening, as we had a full moon to ride by at night. The paralysis of the hands and arms, from which both Mrs. McIlrath and myself had been acute sufferers, came over me again at Ogden, and caused a week's stop instead of a day. I consulted a physician, who imperatively ordered that I take a course of treatment at Utah Hot Springs, situated ten miles out of Ogden. Before we entered into our week's seclusion, a number of the representative wheelmen of Ogden were determined that we should visit the greatest of all Utah resorts, "The Hermitage," in Ogden Canyon. On Tuesday, June 25, a party comprising Mr. and Mrs. W. Beardsley, Mr. and Mrs. F. Sherwood, F. C. Scramm, Editor Thomas of the Press, J. W. Warner and the Inter Ocean tourists rode slowly up the steep grades into the rocky boundaries of the Canyon. "The Hermitage" is a sequestered little house, five miles up the gorge, ensconced in a natural cleft in the mountain side, and facing upon the rushing, foaming Ogden River. We rode to "The Hermitage" without a stop. Standing in the doorway in his shirt sleeves, arms akimbo, was the famous "Billy" Wilson. In all Ogden there is not a character so well known as "Billy" Wilson. He is a brawny Scot, with a sun-burned face, clear blue eyes and a luxuriant growth of sandy hair and whiskers, and he possesses the most charming dialect that was ever imported from the unconquered land of the thistle. I did not at all mind my week as an invalid, for I had eight hours a day aside from my treatment by a physician to devote to sight-seeing. There was but one disagreeable feature in connection with the sojourn at Utah Hot Springs, and that was, the loss of "Tommy Atkins." For his own reasons, which he explained to me, Tommy decided to go it alone, and he left on June 26 to pedal his way alone to the Golden Gate.

The Inter Ocean cyclists left Ogden on July 2, putting in to Corinne for the night. Corinne is distinctive in Utah as strictly a Gentile town, the sight of a mormon at any time being rare. The morning of the great and glorious Fourth, Mrs.

McIlrath and I started from Corinne to celebrate the day with a long run over the sandy plains. As we crossed the tracks in front of the hotel and turned into the smooth road leading to Blue Creek a freight train started from the depot a few rods back of us. The morning was cool, and calling to my wife to keep my rear wheel in sight, I set out to hold that freight train level as long as possible. I had been informed that a chain of foothills that loomed up like a bank of blue fog in the distance, was seven miles away, and as the grade was up, I was determined to lead the engineer a merry dance ere we tipped over the hill and gravity helped the iron horse in his race against my steel-tubed speeder. Over the road we flew, the chug-chug of the engine growing fainter, until we lost it altogether. I knew this was only the start, and bending over my handle-bars I sent my wheel along with a whir. Mrs. McIlrath held on nobly, and when three and a half miles had been covered, the engine was still beyond our hearing. We kept on "jumping on the pedals" and when we tipped over the hills, seven miles from Corinne, the sound of the locomotive's exhaust was barely audible. With the grade in our favor we fairly made things hum. My cyclometer ticked with a continuous rattle like an old-fashioned watchman's signal. And now the engineer of the train seemed to enter into the spirit of the race. He tooted short blasts at us as he gained ground and his train caught the impetus afforded by the grade. The crew also took part in the fun, and from the top of the cars and caboose, they gave us the "come-on" signals when the little red coach tripped around the curve like the last flame of a shooting star. And then we were alone on the desert of Western Utah.

Seven miles further on, we came to the end of the main ditch of the Bear River Canal Company. There we met a gang of men who reported having met "Tommy Atkins" nine days ahead. This was the first tidings we had received of the merry Englishman, and it was most welcome news. The exciting ride of the day caused us to forget that it was the Nation's birthday, until we passed Bradley's Ranch and gazed upon the Stars and Stripes gayly floating from a tall staff in front of his house. Bradley saluted us, and in reply to our question if we might send any news of him to friends in the East, he proudly answered: "Tell them that Old Glory waves over Bradley's Ranch the same as it does over the postoffice in Chicago on the Fourth of July." I had calculated upon spending the night at Kelton. We arrived there for supper and found the one hotel of the town in undisputed possession of a gang of cowboys, who were celebrating the Fourth in approved Western style. Whisky was tapped by the barrel, and there were indications of a beer famine soon to come. The men were good-natured for the most part, but so noisy with their fun that Mrs. McIlrath concluded Kelton was no place for her, and we moved on in the direction of a ranch where we had been told we might be accommodated with lodging. I was three hours cruising around the plains trying to find this ranch, and had almost come to the opinion that no such place existed. The moon had gone down and it was difficult riding in the dark. I ran into what I considered an embankment, and was thrown from my wheel, then the embankment gave a loud snort and a scream from Mrs. McIlrath behind let me know that she had also been in a collision. We had struck in the blackness a herd of cows, all lying down and peacefully chewing their cuds. This I took as evidence that the ranch was a reality, and again I began the search for the house, this time riding squarely into a barb-wire fence. Following the line of the wire I came to the dwelling, a prosperous-looking abode, painted and adorned with a veranda and curtains in the window. All knocks and calls were unanswered, which led me to believe that the family could be not far away, probably attending a Fourth of July celebration in the vicinity. Mrs. McIlrath and I sat down on a log to await their return. After an hour's silent vigil, my watch told me that it was long after midnight. The air had grown raw and the wind chilling. I built a fire in the front yard and made a place for Mrs. McIlrath to lie down. To those of my readers who have tried to sleep before a camp fire without blanket Mrs. McIlrath's discomfort will be readily understood. I curled up behind her, doing as best I could to keep off the wind, and thus she was enabled to derive several hours' slumber, but as for myself, I was almost frozen when I waked at five the next morning, and learned that the family had been absent over night. By this time I was desperate, and with one of my small pistols I bowled over two fat chickens that were cackling around the yard. I was ready, had I been surprised by the owner, to pay liberally for the pullets, and consequently I felt no sting of conscience for my tramp-like behavior. The fire was replenished, and while Mrs. McIlrath dressed the chickens in a crude fashion, picking them in hot water boiled in a tin can which I had found on the back porch, I skirmished the premises in hopes of digging up some old utensil of the kitchen with which to cook them. I could find nothing, but my inventive mind, the same which prompted me to patch a tire with a buckskin glove, came to the rescue when my eyes alighted on a piece of stovepipe. It was old and rusted and had been thrown away evidently months before. I smashed its circular shape flat, scraped off the rust, and that served as our frying pan. For breakfast that morning, we had fried chicken, not cooked Maryland style, to be sure, but nevertheless sufficient to stave off hunger until noon. The family had still not yet returned, as we prepared to leave, and telling Mrs. McIlrath that we would be far away when their anger exploded and that we, ourselves, would never be suspected, the blame for the depredation doubtless being placed upon the shoulders of some unfortunate hobo, we mounted our wheels and steered away in the direction of the Nevada State Line. I was unable to learn the name of the people at whose ranch we had stopped and whose chickens I had appropriated, but if they should ever come across this book, I should like them to know that our intentions were honest at least, and that we should have paid for our breakfast could we have met anybody to take the money.

By looking at our cyclometers we ascertained that eighty-four miles had been covered on the Fourth of July. We had hard riding the next day, arriving at Lucin at 11 o'clock at night. For once in the life of somebody, a little intemperance served a good purpose. The section boss at Lucin lived alone in a neat cottage, with his Italian and Chinese laborers in quarters a couple of hundred yards away. The section boss, whose name is of no consequence here, had celebrated the Fourth too vigorously. The depression which followed and the loneliness of his surroundings had thrown him into a state of nervousness that made him jump like a man shot if one but snapped his fingers behind him. The sight of company was the best medicine he could have had, and before we had an opportunity to ask him for shelter, he had overwhelmed us with an invitation to come in and stay—stay a week if we only would. We came to Nevada on July 6, with a register of 2,283 miles to our credit, made since leaving the office of the Inter Ocean. This represented a daily average of 57½ miles. At Tecoma, our first stopping place in the state, we found an inquisitive crowd awaiting us. As the crowd was in Tecoma, so it proved to be throughout Nevada. Everywhere the people understood fully who we were, where we were from and the auspices under which we journeyed, but we had difficulty in convincing them that we were not dead-broke and that we were not touring the globe for a wager. There have been so many queer trips recently made by men who start out penniless to receive thousands of dollars upon the culmination of their journey that the public, I noted, had grown to expect all sorts of hard luck stories from tourists whose mode of travel was any other than the railroad. But for all their suspicions of us, they were indulgent and good-natured, and never once were we mistreated or insulted. Nevada also gave us the hardest work in moving through the United States. The sands and head-winds were fifty per cent more exhausting than the distances, and the 132 miles we made the day we entered Denver did not tire us one-half as much as the 61 miles we covered on July 7, the day we rode into Halleck.

CHAPTER V.

HALTED BY VIGILANTES AND AN ESCAPE FROM LYNCHING IN NEVADA—A DELIGHTFUL RECEPTION AT RENO—ON THE STEAMER FOR JAPAN.

The morning of July 8 we set forth for Elko, twenty-six miles away. Mrs. McIlrath and I were moving along at a good gait, when a band of horsemen overtook us near Osina. They dashed across our path and dismounted simultaneously, closing in upon us. The leader approached me with a command to open my mouth and display my teeth. I thought it was a joke and demanded to know who was the dentist in the party. "None of your nonsense," growled the leader, "let's see your teeth." My jaws immediately flew back as far as nature would permit and the leader looked down my throat searchingly. "No, boys; 'taint Brady," he called, and then it was my time to do some talking. Their explanation in brief was that they were hunting for one Brady, a bandit who had been running wild throughout for weeks. He was about my size, they said, quite as likely to be dressed as a wheelman as anything else, and the sole unfailing marks of identification in their possession were the gold fillings in his molars. Goodness knows, what would have happened to me had I been the owner of many gold-plugged teeth. I might have been shot on the spot, or lynched, or at any rate dragged to jail with days of delay and humiliation before me ere I could make myself properly known. We put in a day and a night at Elko and resumed the journey on Wednesday, July 10. The first six miles of going outside of Elko were as good as any Eastern roads I have ever traveled, but the white dust which fills the air makes it advisable for all tourists to ride with gloves and their caps well down upon the head. When this dust mingles with perspiration on any exposed part of the body it smarts and burns like a powerful acid. Our tires suffered also and one by one the punctures repaired in Salt Lake City began to let go. Every revolution brought out a hiss like an angry serpent. By pumping every half mile we managed to get into Golconda on July 12, having made 24 miles in seven and a half hours, the hardest traveling we had yet known. It was 20 miles further to Winnemucca, which we covered easily next day, halting in the town for repairs. On July 17, we were again on the road, leaving Lovelocks, but we could make only three miles an hour in the sand and were forced to return to the station in order to take to the railroad tracks.

Two miles from the Nevada Hot Springs, by riding the railroad trestles, my front wheel played me another one of its tricks and threw me down a twelve-foot embankment. Scrambling back to the trestle, I picked up my wheel with its handle-bars snapped in two. My photographic outfit was spilled and the camera broken. The most expert wheelman cannot ride over Western roads without his handle-bars. I sent Mrs. McIlrath ahead while I gathered up my belongings and pushing the wheel before me, I set out to walk to the section house at Desert, ten miles away. As I journeyed along the railroad tracks, bewailing my plight and rebelling at the three hours' tramp before me, I spied a rusty bolt in the road bed, and it occurred to me that it would prove a good substitute for my broken bars. I lashed it with wire in place and found it answered the purpose admirably. Slow riding was better than walking, but at that I did not make out so poorly, for I lumbered into the section house at Desert only fifteen minutes after Mrs. McIlrath had arrived. Our ride through Nevada was varied. For days, we sped along rough tracks, meeting none but illiterate laborers and camping at night upon the hard dirty floors, often without covering. Meal after meal we partook of without fork or spoon and in many instances, the only knife we had was rusted and mayhap coated with plug tobacco. Table linen, napkins, soap and even hair brushes were often total strangers to us. It seems that the men whom fate has decreed to work in these out-of-the-way places have for an object in life only a place of refuge from the elements. Then again maybe the day after our dinner had been eaten from a dry-goods box in such unpleasant surroundings, we would be at one of the famous health resorts or hunting lodges that abound in the West, and where everything is of the very best quality. The two extremes of life came under our observation within our 1,800 miles out of Chicago.

At Vista, in accordance with a number of telegrams sent us at various points, we were met by Prof. M. E. Wilson and wife on a tandem, heading a welcoming party sent out from Reno. All preparations for our stay in this charming city had been attended to by them before our arrival. Following an advance guard, with Mrs. Wilson and my wife ahead, the Professor and myself closing up the rear of the procession, the party rode down the main streets of Reno and drew up at the Riverside Hotel. A dinner fit for a king and sufficient for a regiment was on the table ready for us. Our hospitable friends, with an eye for our comfort and enormous appetites, declined to delay sitting down any longer than it would take for us to bathe our faces and hands. They remained for an hour or more after we had cleared the table, arranging trips for our entertainment on the next day. For the first time since leaving Chicago Mrs. McIlrath and I were so tired that when we retired we slept soundly until 1 o'clock in the afternoon of the next day. Likely as not we should have slept until the evening had we not been called by A. S. Bragg, editor of the Reno Gazette, and Miss Manning, a charming young lady, whom the editor had brought along as a companion for Mrs. McIlrath. With them we rode over the entire city, the two ladies going ahead, enabling the editor and myself to fall behind and indulge in a discussion of our favorite theme, "Shall it be gold, or free silver at 16 to 1?" July 20, with Professor and Mrs. Wilson we visited the famous mines of Virginia City, and this time we did not go upon bicycles. The Professor called for us in a carriage, whose horses were piloted by a reliable veteran, who had served his apprenticeship on the earlier stage coaches. The ride to Virginia City, up the side of a mountain, is fraught with danger. Only two weeks before our arrival there was a fatal accident, a couple of tourists and their horses being dashed over a precipice, and after I had arrived in San Francisco three weeks later, I learned of the deaths of two ladies and a gentleman, who had undertaken the same trip on horseback, and had met their end in precisely the same manner.

On Monday, July 22, we departed from Reno upon our last relay of American touring for three years. Prof. Wilson rode with us and as we passed Saw Mill Summit, the white dust died away and I saw nothing but flowers, beautiful foliage and waving grass. The Professor calmly remarked: "You have entered a new country; you are now in California." We left Truckee July 23 in the morning, making the 160 miles to Sacramento shortly after dusk. Four days in Sacramento, devoted to sight-seeing, and then we started for San Francisco, arriving there July 29. We had then covered 3,002 3–8 miles from Chicago in 52 days.

A complete overhauling of our wheels and time allowed for necessary shopping by Mrs. McIlrath, caused us to remain in San Francisco much longer than we had anticipated. The days did not hang heavy upon our hands, the wheelmen of the city being universally kind in their attentions to us both. My space is too limited to go into the details attendant upon our sojourn in San Francisco, as much as I should like for my cycling readers to know of the pleasure in store for a wheelman in the metropolis of the Pacific Coast.

On October 12 the telegraph message of three words, "We are off," was flashed to the Inter Ocean office in Chicago. We had taken passage on the Occidental and Oriental Line steamer City of Pekin, bound for Yokohama, the chief city of the flowery kingdom of Japan. Everything for our accommodation that could be done on board the steamer was ordered, not the least of our favors being two seats at the table of Captain Trask, commanding officer of the vessel. Our fellow passengers were an interesting lot, including two United States naval officers; a member of the English Parliament, his wife and a traveling companion; an officer of the Austrian army; two French globe trotters, who intended to write a book of travel upon their return to Paris; a Corean nobleman; four American missionaries, and a mysterious personage whose visiting card read, "Capt. Vladmir Samioloff," of the army of the Czar. The steerage passengers were exclusively Japanese and Chinese. The third day out Capt. Trask escorted me through the steerage and showed me the hospital ward, which contained three Japanese, who were going home to die. The captain explained to me that in every case of the death of a Japanese on board a steamer, the body was given a sailor's burial, but that with the Chinese it was entirely different. The body of a dead Chinaman, even though he were to die one day out, would be embalmed and taken home to his relatives, a Chinese embalmer nearly always being on board a vessel for just such emergencies.

Mrs. McIlrath, for six days out, was the most sea-sick woman that ever tossed in a berth. She was unable to come on deck before Friday, Oct. 18, and rough weather, which set in the next day, sent her below again, and thus she lost one of the prettiest parts of our voyage across the Pacific. Monday, Oct. 21, was the shortest day I ever passed. It lasted, strictly speaking, but seven hours, or from 12 o'clock to 7:15 a. m., at which time the City of Pekin crossed the meridian. Having been constantly racing with the sun, and so gaining time, at 7:16 o'clock we had entered upon Tuesday, Oct. 22. At 11:30 on the morning of the same day we caught our first sight of Japan, the white crest of the sacred mountain, Fujiyama, looming in the distance. Monday evening, Oct. 28, at 8:15 o'clock, the City of Pekin steamed into the harbor, having broken her record thirty-seven minutes. The fact of the boat's arrival ahead of time, made the hours so late before the steam launches of the hotel arrived that we decided to remain on board the steamer until next morning. We were still asleep Tuesday morning when the runners of the hotels roused us by pounding upon our state-room door. The Club Hotel was the one we had selected, and when the representative announced himself, we gave a list of our baggage and hastened to dress. At the English hataba (a long pier running out into the bay) our baggage was thoroughly overhauled by the customs officers, and upon our wheels and camera a duty of five per cent was imposed. As cameras are listed at 50 yen and bicycles at 200 yen each, this would have cost us in duty 22 yen 50 sen, or about twelve dollars in gold. After a short conference and an ostentatious display of Secretary Gresham's passports and the Inter Ocean credentials, which the revenue officers had not understood, our articles were franked and we entered the city.

CHAPTER VI.

JAPAN'S QUEER CREDIT SYSTEM—INTER OCEAN TOURISTS AT
THE BURIAL OF PRINCE KITASHIRAKAWA—A POINT FOR
ALL AMERICANS.

The Club Hotel, which is the headquarters for American tourists and residents, is situated only a block from the pier and adjacent to the Consulates, shops and points of interest. The owners and managers are Europeans, or "foreigners" as they are called in Japan, but the service of the hotel is exclusively by natives. Your room is cared for by a "boy," your meals served by a "boy" and "boys," sometimes 50 years of age, perform every possible service. There are without doubt more courtesies shown a guest in Japan than in any other country. Our reception in the city was all that we could ask. The letter to Col. McIvor, American Consul, from friends at his home in Cedar Rapids, Iowa, made us thrice welcome at that gentleman's residence. The fact of our representing an American newspaper made us at home in newspaper circles, which are controlled largely by Americans. Our coming had been heralded to the wheelmen of Japan, and as we were expected some weeks before we arrived, the coming was of more than ordinary interest.

Bicycling, at the time of my visit, was just beginning to become popular in Japan, and what machines were used were imported at great cost from the States and Europe. But with commendable enterprise the manufacturers of Japan now perfect their own machines, all parts of which are made and assembled in local concerns, operated by local capital and mechanics. In Japan it is not expected that cash will be tendered for anything purchased or rented, with perhaps the exception of "rickshas," which correspond in their common use to the cabs of American cities, only that they are drawn by "boys" instead of horses. There is an abominable system of credit established in the empire by which all foreigners purchase and temporarily pay for all articles upon bits of memorandum called "chits." If a gentleman in Yokohama wishes a drink, a cigar, new hat or even a suit of clothes, he steps into the nearest place of business adapted to filling his requirements and, after making his purchase, signs a bit of paper, giving date, price and buyer's name and address, and the first of every month the "chit" is sent him as a receipt bill. To a well-appearing foreigner reasonable credit will be extended without question. My knowledge of this system was derived in the most peculiar manner. Mrs. McIlrath and I were touring the shops, when her attention was attracted by a shawl. She entered the shop, priced the article and I advised the purchase, but our pocketbook had been left at the hotel, she blushingly informed me. We thanked the shopman for his trouble and promised to return the same evening. The price was six yen, or about three dollars, as quoted by the dealer, and as we started out of the shop he called to us, asking if the price was too much. I explained our embarrassed condition, and he immediately wrapped up the shawl, placing one of the printed slips upon the counter, asked me to sign a "chit" for five yen. I was an entire stranger, yet upon credit I obtained for one yen less that which I could not purchase for cash. The most astonishing fact connected with this extraordinary system is that no laws are provided to punish dead-beats or frauds.

On Monday, Nov. 11, we journeyed over to Tokio, eighteen miles distant, to witness the funeral ceremonies over the body of His Imperial Highness Prince Kitashirakawa, a commander of the Imperial Guard. In tropical Formosa, under a fierce sun and amid miasmatic jungle, the prince died of malarial fever Oct. 29. The sad news reached Japan shortly after our arrival, but by a curious custom, was not announced to the people as authentic or an accepted fact until officially given out by the imperial authorities on Nov. 5. In fact the Prince officially lived until that time. News of his victories in Formosa brought forth new honors and distinctions, and upon Nov. 2, he, or rather the corpse, was decorated with the Collar of the Chrysanthemum and Grand Cordon of the Imperial Family. The service was simple, yet impressive, without a shade of paganism or superstition. There was much about it also that would befit countries, considering themselves superior to Japan to imitate. One most noticeable was the order of the assembled masses. Not a person offered to step outside of the prescribed limit. There was no jamming or crowding. No voices spoke louder than a whisper, and the presence of police and militia was necessary only as an exhibition of official dignity. Where houses of greater height than one story faced on the line of march, or porches existed above the elevation of the street, the curtains at windows and doors were closely drawn, and the occupants stood in the street. No yelling, gesticulating mob filled the telegraph and telephone poles and roofs, for it is not permissible in Japan that anyone look down upon the funeral of a dignitary. The passage of the Emperor through the streets calls into effect the same condition. He may be viewed from an equal level, but never looked down upon from an elevation.

TRYING FOR INFORMATION ON THE ROAD.—SEE PAGE 25.

I am glad to record that it is a mistaken impression that there exists in Japan a general feeling against Europeans and Americans. In any part of the Mikado's realm the American is as safe as at home and the European is comparatively as secure. Why is this distinction of a degree made? During the late chastisement which Japan administered to China the action was so one-sided that it could scarcely be called war. As soon as the Russians interfered, threats were made by a few anarchistic extremists in Yokohama, Tokio and other large cities, against the "white man" and his property. The simple minds of the rabble of oriental nations do not regard the English, French, Russian and German subjects as belonging to distinctive nations, but classify them as the "white man." The ministers and consuls at Tokio, during this excitement, were brought under guard to Yokohama. Their residences were guarded by police, and when any of these gentlemen drove out in carriages, they were surrounded by detectives, who were compelled to use force for the passages of their vehicles through the streets. Not an act of violence occurred which reflected upon the local government in the slightest degree, but the satisfactory ending of threatened murder and riot was due entirely to the vigilance of the secret service department. Upon the other hand, when the United States Consul drove out there was no necessity of a guard. A sight of the peerless colors of the United States emblazoned on the carriage door, or the unmistakable uniform of the driver, and the sea of humanity which filled the street would part, and with bows and cheers, allow our representative to go his way. Policemen and officers saluted with caps in hand, while perhaps only a half square away the guard of one of the other consuls struggled fiercely with an unyielding mob. That is the reason I say an American is as safe from personal interference in any part of Japan as in the heart of any of our great cities. An Englishman is, in fact, more secure here than he would be in any of the acquired provinces of Great Britain.

The short rides of the Inter Ocean cyclists, taken in and about Yokohama, Kanagarua, Mississippi Bay and Tokio, demonstrated to us the truth that the Japanese have not only respect, but love for the Yankee. The roads of Japan compare favorably with the boulevards of American cities, except in matter of width. They are smooth, hard and upon the sea coast quite level. One of the finest courses I have ridden over is a six-mile run we took daily before breakfast in Yokohama. The course begins at the Club Hotel, along the Bund to the Yalo Bashi, following this to the Haz-Aso-No Bashi and from there to Mississippi Bay, the Bluffs and back to the hotel.

The Inter Ocean tourists left Yokohama Monday, Nov. 18, having secured new passports for the interior, where the treaty laws do not extend protection or privileges to the foreigner. Our destination was unknown even to ourselves, but as we were astride our wheels it mattered little where we wound up, so long as interesting scenery and incidences were daily occurrences. One point, in main, was to form the center of a circle around which we intended to swing, and that center was Fujiyama, the sacred mountain. To reach the lower slopes of Fuji there are many pathways, but for cyclists there is but one that may be practicably adopted, and that by way of Gotenba, Yamanka and Yoshida, "the route of temples," the course traveled by the native pilgrims to Fuji in summer months. We took a southwesterly direction from Yokohama and came to a well ballasted wagon road, running almost parallel with the railroad, connecting Tokio with Kobe, 400 miles south. We passed through the villages of Fujisawa, Hiratsuka and Oisa, crossing the River Vanugawa, and entering Kodsu, a village of large proportions, at noon. Kodsu is about thirty miles from Yokohama, and it was here we had hoped to eat our lunch and find drinking water in which we could place confidence. The one drawback to tourists in the interior of Japan is water. In their natural condition the waters are pure, cool streams, coursing down snow-clad mountains, miles in the interior, but passing through the villages, their course is diverted into ditches and water-boxes, running through the gutters and sometimes under the houses of the town. The sewerage of surface drains empties into these streams. Cooking utensils and food are washed, fish are cleaned and even dogs drink from and bathe in these gutters. The same system of water supply exists in all of Japan, and after we had struck Kodsu, Mrs. McIlrath and I drank only native-made beer during our stay in the land of the Mikado.

At 1 o'clock we were again on the road, keeping with the railroad tracks until we passed through Sakawagawa. Little was to be seen but rice and vegetable fields, the mountains in the distance and the swift rushing river coursing to the sea. We covered 72 miles by 7 o'clock, arriving at Gotenba, where we spent our first night in a Japanese yadoyo, or inn. In a Japanese sleeping apartment there is nothing to be seen as one enters the room except matting upon the floor. There is not a table, chair, bed or any other article of furniture visible. We had begun to think that we were to pass the night on the floor as we had done in the section houses of Nevada, when an attendant entered the room, bearing cushions, and a second one came with a table, small affairs resembling unpadded foot-rests, braziers with live coals and tiny bronze tea-kettles. The cushions were piled into soft heaps about fourteen inches high, the tables placed between, and we were motioned to a seat upon the cushions. To the right and left were placed box-like trays and in these our food was served in dainty bowls and dishes. At 9 o'clock, when I thought it time to retire, I clapped my hands for a servant. To the girl who answered I made known my wishes and she called two assistants, who appeared, each bringing a pair of padded comforters. The comforters were spread upon the matting in layers, and at the head of each was placed the Japanese substitute for a pillow, a box six inches square by twelve inches long, the upper edge slightly padded. We passed a most comfortable night, and awakened only by the maid entering our room with a tea set. After breakfast we called for our bill and the amount rendered was two yen, or one dollar in gold. Bed, bath, breakfast and supper, unequaled service and every attention in a first-class inn to be had at the rate of sixty cents a day! By 9 o'clock we were again on the road with Fujiyama looming up thirty miles away. From the guide, who had previously given us instructions, we knew which course to take, and so turned up the fork apparently leading to the very root of the mountain. We did not stop at Yamanaka village, but rode through the main streets, astounding the natives and passing from their view, before they realized what had happened, except that something unseen or unheard of before in Yamanaka had passed their way. From Yamanaka to Yoshida our path was over level, smooth roads, but in the latter place we were compelled to stop and consult our guide-books and the police. At the police station, before we were given any information, our passports were demanded. I produced mine, but Mrs. McIlrath had left hers, the most necessary of her effects, behind. The officer looked over my papers and then pointed to my wife. The passports had been made separately at our request, and of course mine made no mention of Mrs. McIlrath. To gain time and collect my wits I took the paper from the officer's hands and glanced over the copy attached, which was written in English. An idea "struck" me. My name was "parted in the middle;" why not give my wife half of it? Calling the attention of the official to the English copy, I pointed to "H. Darwin," and then to my wife. Then laying my finger upon the name "McIlrath," I patted myself on the chest. The official referred to the Japanese copy, I repeated the pantomime, he smiled and bowed, and making a few mystic characters upon the passport, he altered it to read, "H. Darwin, female, and McIlrath, male."

CHAPTER VII.

A NIGHT IN A JAPANESE TEMPLE—UNSUCCESSFUL ATTEMPT TO "KODAK" THE MIKADO—LANDED AMONG THE "HEATHEN CHINEE."

The sun was setting when we left Yoshida, and with our path principally composed of the narrow dikes separating the rice fields, progress was painfully slow. Miyhoji, seven miles away, was our destination for the night. We had an idea that Miyhoji was a village, and so clicked off eight miles before we discovered that we had either passed the town or were on the wrong track. About one mile back we had seen a light and there we returned. We were at Miyhoji, one of the historic old temples of Japan, and there we slept. The priest lived here with his wife and two acolytes, and a cordial welcome it was they gave us. At 5 o'clock on the afternoon of Nov. 20, we entered a forest at the end of Lake Mishi-No-Umi. We had six miles yet to go ere we sighted Shoji Lake and the hotel at that point kept by Y. Hoshino, a naturalized Japanese gentleman, who was born in Scotland, and having lived eighteen years on the islands of Japan, finally became an adopted citizen. Traveling the forests at night in Japan over lava beds with path illumed only by a cycle lamp is not the most pleasant of journeys. The narrow way is uncertain, deep chasms appear upon either side and I had several rocky falls. I was bruised and battered when we came to Hoshino's residence and lost no time in taking to my bed. At daybreak our host called us to view the silent volcano rising in grandeur to the extreme height 12,365 feet. There is not a peak in all the grand elevation of the Rockies that can compare with Fuji. Pike's Peak, taken from its setting of lesser lights, which but serve to destroy its beauty, and placed upon the plains of Illinois, would not even prove a petty rival to the one before us. As we looked upon Fuji that morning a spotless mantle of snow cowled her crest, the scintillations of which formed a halo of prismatic light about her, and it did not seem strange to realize that the natives worshiped this wondrous monument of eruptive power and beauty.

It was our good fortune to be present at the greatest of all "war holidays" held at Shokausha Park in Kudan, on Dec. 15, 16, 17 and 18. After leaving Hoshino's we returned to Tokio, and spent the time in touring the vicinity until these great fetes at which the emperor and empress are always present, were held. Dec. 17, the day upon which His Imperial Majesty Metsu Hito, Emperor of Japan, was to appear at Shokousha Park, dawned dull and threatening, and awakened within us the dread idea that the mightiest of all Japanese would not be on view. At the park the attendance was something incalculable. Tokio seemed to have had its million souls augmented by the thousands of Yokohama, Nikko and other surrounding cities.

Our experiences in the vast crowd were paralleled only by those in the dense throng at the World's Fair on Chicago Day. Shortly before 11 o'clock, a tremor ran through the crowd, then a hoarse murmur, and amid a cavalcade of gay lancers, the carriage of the emperor swept through the lane of blue-coated soldiers, and halted directly in front of where we were standing. As the emperor turned and looked about him, I saw a Japanese of low stature, dressed in the uniform of the commander of the army and navy; his dark-complexioned face partly shaded by a peculiar hat, heavily jeweled. The photographs of the Mikado represent him to be a slender man, with a long face, but they are not true likenesses. The Mikado has a round, full face, high intellectual temple, a black mustache which droops over the gentle, pleasing mouth, and with soft eyes, inexpressibly sad, his face appeals to one as that of a man suffering under the royal chains which confine him to the narrow limits of the palace grounds.

He stood but a moment in the roadway and surrounded by nobles of various high degrees with bowed form, he moved up the graveled path, ascended the steps of the temple and disappeared within. While he was at worship my American instinct to obtain a souvenir of the occasion got the better of my respect for royalty, and I unswung my camera and prepared to make a picture of the scene. Almost directly two pairs of brown hands seized the camera, turned it sharply upward, and held it until the imperial carriage received the person of the emperor and departed. The Mikado was not to be shot at even by a camera. It was a keen disappointment to me, but I learned later that it was better I did not succeed. Had I snapped the picture I should have lost my camera and probably been roughly handled myself. I was told that I had been followed all morning by the police, who knew what I would attempt with the instrument, and who were detailed especially to frustrate my plans. My camera was not only excluded here, but in all buildings that held treasures or relics of the government and public departments.

We had spent two months on the volcanic island, our last few days being fraught with interesting episodes and instructive visits. We had received so many courtesies at the hands of the Japanese, both from individuals and government, that we were loathe to leave for the mainland of China. The final courtesy extended me by the Japanese Government was the privilege of visiting the new prison just completed, and as I was the first European granted such permission, I felt bound to accept the unusual invitation. The precautions taken against disease by germ in the penitentiary at Tokio are equal to those practiced in the most famous hospitals and clinics in the United States and Europe. The wards were models of cleanliness, well lighted, well ventilated, warm and comfortable. The industrial features of the institution, I am safe in saying, are superior to those of the vast state prisons in my own country. There were seven workshops devoted respectively to the manufacture of fire engines, to the weaving and spinning of cotton and silk; the manufacture of silk umbrellas; production of steel hairpins; bricks for the city; the weaving of cloth and the manufacture of stockings, and one devoted to all branches of carpentry and wood-carving. The governor of the prison presented us with many valuable mementoes of our visit. But for that matter, every Japanese gentleman of rank whom we visited sent us a little souvenir of our meeting. We were compelled to purchase additional trunks in which to store our "curios," and when we left on Jan. 12, 1896, on the City of Pekin, for China, we were forced to have our "excess baggage" shipped to our home in America.

When the Inter Ocean cyclists reached Shanghai, one of the first sights we wished to see was the people among whom we were to travel for the next 2,000 miles of our trip, and we wished to see them at home. To view them in all their glory as an uncivilized, barbaric race, a trip to the old city was necessary, and on this errand Mrs. McIlrath and I started Jan. 25. We had intended to ride our wheels, but were dissuaded from doing so on account of the hindrance they would prove in sight-seeing. Our friends strongly urged that we take a guide, claiming it unsafe for foreigners to walk about the city alone, but as we were perforce to travel in Chinese territory far less accustomed to "foreign devils" than the inhabitants of Shanghai, we resolved to make our initial bow among the vegetarians unprotected, save by our nerve and a stout cane. Crowds gathered around us wherever we stopped. When I pulled out my notebook and fountain pen, the masses literally fought for places near in order to see me write, and when I had finished and upheld the scrawled page for them to look at, a roar of laughter went up, and several pointed to Chinese characters upon the dead walls of a temple, and in pantomime asked if the ink tracings on the page represented writing. The task of getting away from the crowd was much more difficult than forming it, and we were escorted the remainder of the afternoon by a monster band of chattering idlers.

In many of the shops passed we noticed little girls, mere babies they were, standing on stools or leaning over railings, their heads on their arms. The poor tots moaned constantly, their little tear-stained faces depicting anguish seldom seen on the bright faces of children. Nothing seemed to attract their attention, nothing pleased them, and little wonder. Their tiny feet had been bound in unyielding rolls of cloth since the day they were born, and already the bones and sinews were crushing each other into a mass of unrecognizable pulp, held together only by the skin and bandages. This practice is common among the Chinese of all classes and produces the fashionable small foot of the women. The bandages once placed on are never removed, except to be replaced by others, and in result, hundreds of lives are sacrificed annually, the children's feet mortifying and sloughing away. It is erroneous to believe that only women of high caste have small feet. I saw women whose feet were only two and a half and three inches long, dragging drays.

For four hours we wandered through the dark alleyways and streets, passing through tunnels and archways that were filled with noxious vapors and used by the public for all manner of nuisances. We experienced no interference with our progression, the only hostile feeling being shown was by a few street arabs who pelted us with stones and fruit skins. This treatment would be accorded a Chinese by our own precious youth in the States and does little harm if no attention is paid to the offenders. Dogs made several attacks upon us, but the little ammonia gun I always carry effectually checked all onslaughts and filled the observing Chinese with wonder. The "gun" was one of my own manufacture, simply a rubber bulb with a short glass nozzle. The bulb I kept filled with ammonia, and when dogs annoyed me, either on my wheel or afoot, the bulb, concealed in the hand, with the nozzle projecting between the fingers, made a most effective weapon. Directing the nozzle in the dog's direction, a slight pressure sent a tiny stream into the yelping cur's mouth and eyes. The dog's violent breathing invariably caused him to take a full inhalation before he was aware of the evil designs upon him, and the effect was instantaneous. He would close his mouth with a snap and then perform a wild side somersault on his back. Several times I used the gun upon dogs in Shanghai and did it in such a manner as to conceal the act. The masters of the animals, who stood grinning while the brutes yelped and snapped at us, were unable to comprehend the reason for Fido's acrobatic feats, and in each instance after looking the dog over to find some injury, laughed heartily, and addressed to us words in reference to the dog which were no credit to man's most faithful friend.

CHAPTER VIII.

INTER OCEAN CYCLISTS GUESTS AT A CHINESE WEDDING—
TORTURES OF A NATIVE PRISON REVEALED—JOLLY CELE-
BRATION OF THE NEW YEAR.

The statement made by someone that man's birth, marriage and death are the three important epochs in his brief career, find support in the custom of the Chinese. Births are heralded by fireworks, fetes and rejoicings, and weddings and funerals are marked by lavish outlay of money and great display. The wedding of a Chinese woman is a complicated affair, but is conducted upon the same principles as are the weddings of the American Indians. The bride marries into the groom's family, not the groom into the bride's family; the wedding occurs at the groom's home and the presents are his property. Although a Chinese may marry as many wives as his income will permit him to support, the first wife is the only one that has an extensive ceremony performed over the nuptials, the succeeding wives entering the life of the husband with as little ceremony as a domestic or a new piece of furniture. In fact as such the additional wives are regarded, being bartered for and bought like merchandise. Mrs. McIlrath and I were fortunate in being present at the elaborate wedding ceremony of a Chinese couple. I fancy that if some of my American friends had their wedding march played by a Chinese orchestra, they would be taken from the altar raving lunatics. A boiler yard or a saw mill would not take "show money" with a Chinese wedding orchestra as a peace disturber. But with all the queer ideas dominant in China, there are a few very sound customs and laws, one, particularly, governing marriage and the duties involved. It may be said truthfully that no race of people on earth possess more loyal wives than the Chinese. Infidelity is punishable by horrible death, and even the mildest of flirtations is a serious offense and a pastime unknown among the more gentle sex of China. The women, though occupying a low plane in the estimate of their liege lords, are devoted to their husbands and homes, laboring zealously for the welfare of their rising generations, but are repaid only by condescending approbation and often neglect. Among the men, the rules of morality are more lax, and the time spent among the slaves, bought of depraved fathers, is limited only by the husband's income and leisure from the absorbing occupation of money-getting.

We sought the darkest side of life in China and found in it all the barrenness, yet hideous cunning, ferocity and cruelty of the middle ages. The foreign concessions of Shanghai are guarded by municipal police, composed of Chinese, Europeans and Indians (Sepoys or Seiks), and these minions of the law are controlled by a superintendent, captain and corps of inspectors. The headquarters of the municipal government, police and other departments are located in a large brick building on the Foo Chow Road, and toward the edifice Mrs. McIlrath, a Mr. Burton, an Englishman, who had joined us, and myself directed our steps on Feb. 12. We were met by Superintendent McKenzie and Inspector Ramsey, both gentlemen who had served Great Britain for many years in various capacities as crime suppressors, and they at once showed us the workings of the system as applied in China. Mr. Ramsey placed a Chinese detective at our service to accompany us to one of the native prisons of the old city. Our guide was Kin Lung, a silk-robed, long-cued celestial, who spoke English fluently and smoked cigarettes incessantly. He was the best we could have selected, and thoroughly did he perform his duties. We entered the city by a route never selected by professional guides to conduct tourists, and passed through alleys and streets where the presence of foreigners was as strange a sight as in the far interior. There were few prisoners in durance on that day, as the morrow was the Chinese New Year and all who could obtain bail had been released for the occasion. Those who remained were pacing back and forth in the long, steel-rod cages which formed a sort of outside porch to each row of cells. Each prisoner was bound to a mate by a long chain, riveted to a steel band about his waist. The interior of the prison was dark, gloomy and foul. The floor was covered with damp straw and no light found its way into this tomb, save through the bars at the front door. There were more than two hundred prisoners confined here, a building 15 × 60 feet, and not a bed, blanket or bench to be seen. Food was not furnished, not even uncooked rice, the incarcerated ones being fed by friends upon the outside and by the charitable visitors.

The execution and punishment ground was next visited and entered by a small door at the back end of the jail. The area was simply a clayed-floor space, one end devoted to a canopied stand from which the officials viewed the punishment. Stakes and pillars standing upright in the soil told of horrors often perpetrated in the name of justice, and at one side was a bamboo fence inclosure, which concealed something I divined was of import. When I started for this inclosure a warning call from the jailer notified me not to attempt to approach nearer, but tossing him a silver piece I walked behind the fence. I beheld an iron cage about ten feet square, in which hung a half naked coolie. His head was held upright by a chain about his neck, and his cue was fastened to the bars above. His body was supported by an iron bar, upon which he sat astride, but to each foot was attached a bamboo basket which contained a heavy load of bricks. The arms were outstretched by chains, fastened to the sides of the cage, and these were drawn taut by twisting them with a bamboo pole. At first sight I thought the man was dead. The tendons on the back of the legs and under the knees stood out in rigid lines; the abdomen was caved in, and in sharp outlines the ribs and chest bones looked as if covered with parchment; the face, yellow in color, was deathly, the eyes sunken, the lips purple and the lower jaw dropped. As I glanced at this horrible sight I called to my wife to keep away. At the sound of my voice, the eyelids of the tortured wretch raised slowly. For a moment the gaze seemed to rest upon us, and the parched and swollen lips made an effort to form some words. Then the lids fell heavily, as if in despair. The body had given up its fight against death, and the soul had departed on its long journey.

In less than two months the Inter Ocean cyclists were participants in the celebration of three distinct New Years, the Japanese New Year, on Dec. 25; the Christian on Jan. 1, and the Chinese celebration on Feb. 13. There is no greater holiday in China than the first day of the year. So religiously are the festivities observed that the natives put aside their absorbing passion of money-earning and all business ceases on the night of Feb. 12, until the morning of the 20th. Shops, even to the cigar, drug and candy stores, close, and supplies for house, ship and hotel must be purchased beforehand to last a week. Vessels which arrive must remain in port, for custom-house and consulate are closed, and as for loading and unloading, the lowest coolie would feel insulted if a gold dollar were offered him for an hour's work during the festal week. The holiday garb of men and women is beyond my power to describe, but this pen picture of one lady of fashion whom we saw, is by Mrs. McIlrath, and I think it worthy of reproduction:

"She was extremely pretty," says Mrs. McIlrath, "just like a fantastic doll. She was painted a dead white, her cheeks tinted pink, her lips brightly reddened and her eyebrows penciled black. Her eyes were as dark and pretty as a baby's. Her hair was smoothed back from her forehead and descending in a curve in front of her ears, was coiled neatly in a polished ball at one side on the back. Around the upper part the coil was a coronet of tiny white flowers, and fastening the coils were four ivory stick-pins. Six little ornaments of tinsel danced from gilt pins thrust in her hair, and large gold and jade earrings were fastened in her ears. Her blouse was beautiful. The body was of blue brocaded satin, with a collarette of gold and silver braid stitched upon yellow silk, which fell like a cape, and the sleeves, cut large and loose, were ornamented to the elbow with the same beautiful designs. Her trousers were of pale pink satin with apple-green figures, and her tiny shoes, no longer than my finger, were of blue satin with ermine around the borders at the top. She had fully a dozen bracelets on one arm and bells on her ankles. Her gloves were of black silk, fingerless mitts, the back stitched with gold wire in beautiful scrolls, and her umbrella was carried by two servants."

Our Chinese passports from Pekin arrived on March 1, and from the date of their reception till the time we left China, I ceased to be H. Darwin McIlrath, becoming Mo Chee Sah, at least so the impressive document stated, with all the rights and privileges of a low-class Chinese mandarin. The letter from Minister Denby, which accompanied the passport, advised me to go exclusively by that name and use while in the Empire the Chinese form of card printed in Chinese characters. Accordingly I visited a Chinese printer, presented my passport and asked that he print me an appropriate card. The next day a coolie left at our room a package of red paper slips, each two and a half by six inches, bearing three black characters. They were my "visiting cards." On inquiry it developed that this was the proper fashion.

The passport was written upon a sheet of coarse paper three by four feet in size, the characters being traced in black and red ink, the edges profusely decorated with signatures of Pekin officials. In the center was a column of characters representing cities and towns, around which a red circle was painted. The cities inside and touched with the circle were those I had permission to visit. Those outside were excluded. We had been long enough in China to learn of the lamentable lack of hotels and inns in the interior. Knowing that for the most part we should have to carry our own bedding and food, we purchased and added to the outfit with which we left Chicago two flannel blankets, a shallow frying pan, a tin plate, which also formed a cover to the frying pan, a knapsack and canteen. My "battery" of three guns was augmented by a double-barrel hammerless shotgun, the barrels and stock of which were sawed off, and, in addition, I carried a short, heavy knife resembling the Cuban machete. A case of beef tea had a place in our luggage, and as we had an abundance of an American brand of malted milk already with us, we were assured that we would pass no such hungry days as we often experienced in our ride to the Pacific Coast.

The afternoon of March 3 Mrs. McIlrath and I mounted our luggage-laden wheels, and, after shaking hands with friends, rolled out upon the broad Bund upon the third stage of our long ride. By March 6 we were a hundred miles from the civilized coast, and already we appreciated the fact that our journey across the walled empire would not be "a thing of beauty and a joy forever." The cries of the natives as they caught sight of us silently gliding by on our wheels was strange. The first impression they received from the unusual sight seemed that of super-stitious dread. Not a few were angry and made threatening gestures, pointing in the direction of Shanghai, as if warning us to turn back. Our cyclometers showed the distance to be 28 miles when our first difficulty presented itself. It was that of a wide and deep creek, without bridge and without ferry. After a quarter of an hour spent in exploring the banks in vain search for the boatman, we came across a house-boat hidden in the brush. It was owned by two French gentlemen, who were having a pleasure ride as far as Su Chow. Canals are the highways of China, and in going overland from place to place, one must follow these filthy, stagnant streams. Our friends from France, with the politeness and courtesy characteristic of their nation, invited us to become their guests upon the house-boat as far as Su Chow, assuring us that the journey on wheel was almost impossible. The Inter Ocean tourists boarded the trim craft, their wheels stowed forward, and relieving their backs of the blankets and luggage, made themselves at home.

Our hosts had had considerable experience in China shooting and trading, and with anecdote of adventure and travel the time passed rapidly until the supper hour. An expert Chinese cook prepared a hearty meal of duck, pheasant and bam-boo sprouts, and after an hour's smoking Mrs. McIlrath retired to the only "state room" on board, while the owners of the boat and I, rolled up in blankets, slept on the floor of the cabin. The coolies towing the boat did not cease their labors until after 10 o'clock, and as they resumed towing before daylight, when I woke at 7 the next morning we had covered almost 30 miles. Breakfast over, with our hosts we took a short walk on the banks of the canal, made a few side trips into the brush, and returned to the boat enriched by a dozen pigeons and a pheasant. After our re-turn to the boat I brought forth the great red-sealed document which the Chinese magistrate had given me in Shanghai, and asked if any of the natives in the crew could decipher the purport of the document as written on the envelope. It was this document which had caused us to travel by way of Su Chow, otherwise we should have taken steamer to Chin Kiang, about 60 miles up the Yang-tse-kiang proper, and there begun our ride. I had inquired at Shanghai of foreigners acquainted with the Chinese mandarin language, but all I could learn was that the document was addressed to the Toa Foi at Su Chow, and friends advised me to deliver it. The mystery did not please Mrs. McIlrath, but after deliberation I decided to take chances. Su Chow is a great dumping ground for criminals, and the document was an order intended to reveal to me more of Chinese customs.

CHAPTER IX.

IN THE AUGUST PRESENCE OF THE TAO TAI—THE PRIVILEGED
GUESTS AT AN EXECUTION—FANATICS PURSUE THE "FOR-
EIGN DEVILS."

At 8 o'clock on the evening of March 4 our boat moored at the locks of the
Grand Canal at Su Chow, but the hour was so late and the streets appeared so
dirty and uncertain, that Mrs. McIlrath and I remained on board until morning.
Su Chow is a typical Chinese city, and our entrance thereto was an event to the
natives. Immediately after breakfast I dispatched a message to the Toa Toi, bearing one of my Chinese cards and the mysterious packet. In an hour the messenger
returned accompanied by four chair bearers and a score of soldiers. They were
to conduct us into the presence of the Toa Toi. The mandarin received us in state
robes, seated upon a high chair, and over his head was held a large umbrella. As
we approached him, he graciously descended from his throne and saluted us with
a low bow. Mr. Charles Lewis, an American trader, acted as interpreter, and as he
spoke Chinese fluently, the mystery of the document and our reception at the palace was soon explained. Mrs. McIlrath and I were not only to see more of Chinese
customs, but were the guests of the mandarin. The document further specified
that we should witness the execution of a woman who had murdered two others
on account of her husband, and at the palace we were to remain until orders came
for the execution. "Seng chee" was the mode of death to which the woman was
sentenced. This meant "thirty-six cuts," so inflicted upon the body as to terribly
mutilate but not prove immediately fatal. The order for execution did not arrive
until March 7. The intervening days, spent in the palace from the time of our arrival, were devoted to our express entertainment, a Chinese boy who spoke English
well having been brought from Shanghai expressly to serve as our interpreter and
guide.

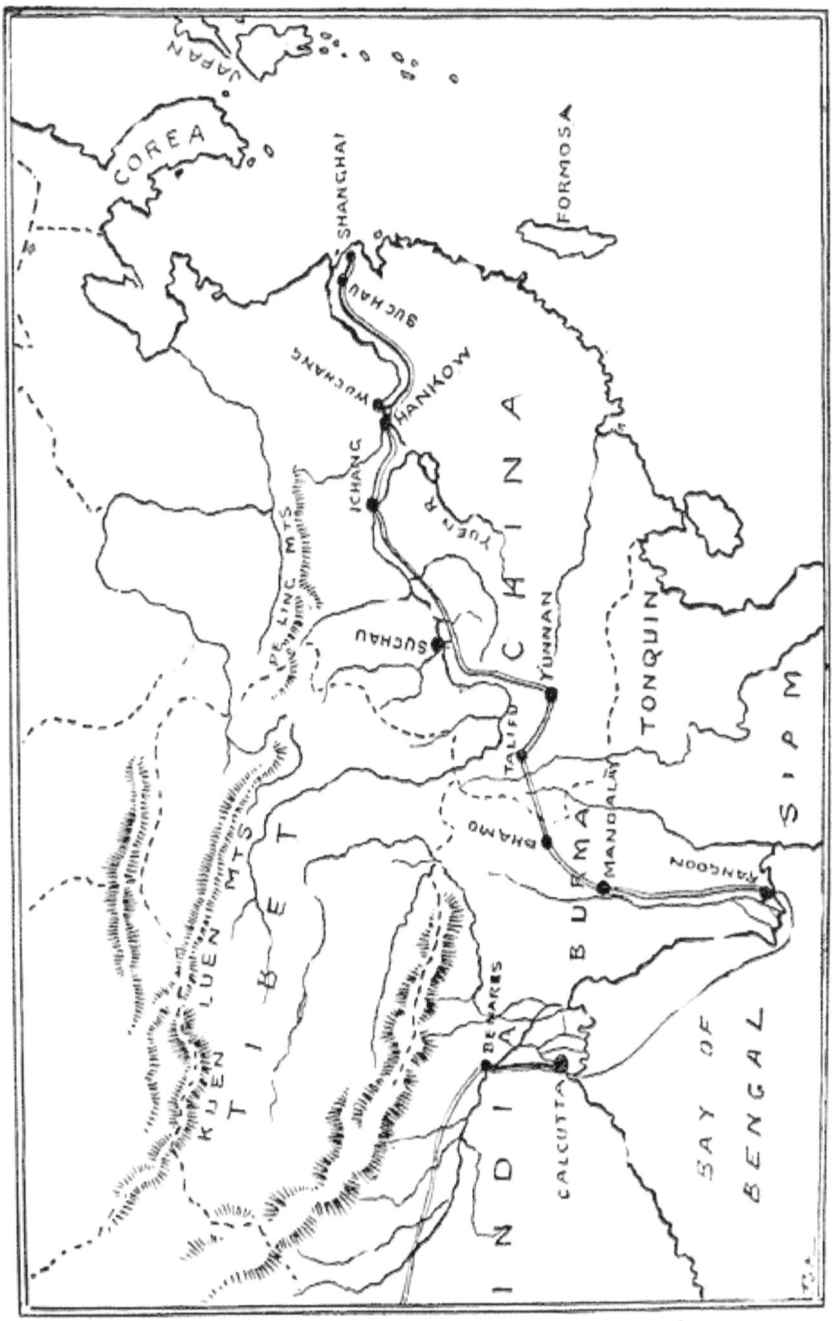

FROM SHANGHAI TO CALCUTTA.

[Outline map showing route of the McIlraths across Asia.]

It was he who awakened us on the morning of the execution with the news that "the papers" had come. Mrs. McIlrath had no wish to view the horrible scene soon to be enacted, and as I left the room she hid her face within her hands and begged me not to mention the proceedings upon my return. The mandarin awaited me in the state room, and with much forethought had ordered two bottles of champagne with which to brace our nerves. A moment later we were on our way to the court yard in the rear of the palace, a retinue of soldiers surrounding us. Two guards dragged the woman directly before the pavilion we occupied. She fell to her knees, and as she beat the ground with her forehead, begging for mercy, the mandarin's secretary read a few words from a scroll, and the poor wretch was sentenced. Two soldiers tied the woman to a post in an upright position, her feet resting upon a heavy block of wood. The white bandage which had bound her forehead was removed and in its place a belt was applied which held her head immovable. The hands were tied behind the post, each one separately. When the preparations were over, the assistant stepped back, and the executioners, like their victim, naked to the waist, and with knives in hand, prostrated themselves at our feet. The chief butcher took his place by the woman's left side, and a knife gleamed. Then one of her ears was thrown upon the ground. A few seconds more and the other ear was sliced In the same manner. Her eyes no longer glanced wildly from side to side, following the movements of her torturers, but appeared fixed upon mine, and, although I could not understand her shrieking cries, I knew she pleaded to me for mercy—a mercy I could not bestow. Her tongue was cut from her mouth, and at each mutilation a secretary told off the number of the slashes. When he counted ten, I braced myself for a glimpse at the sickening sight, and where had been but a few moments before a woman's face, there was but a bloody, unrecognizable ball. With the regularity of a machine the butchers wielded their cleaver. When I next looked it gave me satisfaction to know that death had come to the relief of the wretched woman before the entire thirty-six cuts had been administered.

Before leaving Su Chow we visited the hospital which is conducted under the auspices of the Southern Methodist Episcopal Church. The institution is in charge of Dr. W. H. Park, a typical Southerner, courteous and hospitable, who seemed devoted to his noble work among his heathen patients, and to the medical education of a small class of Chinese students. His corps of assistants included, besides his wife, Dr. Annie Walter, Dr. J. B. Fern, Mr. and Mrs. D. S. Anderson, and the Misses Atkinson, Hearn and Gaither. The cost of sustaining the hospital is paid by the Methodist Mission, but all money derived from patients and from outside visits by Dr. Park, which is considerable, is devoted to the hospital fund.

At Wu Sih we were the guests of Dr. Walters for several days before we departed for Ching Kiang. What few roads China possesses are mere foot paths, and in the Eastern districts, where clay is the principal superficial soil, six months of each year these paths are impassable save to foot passengers. Our appearance, therefore, upon bicycles on roads where the wheelbarrow is the only wheel ever seen, stirred the natives to the wildest pitch. The bicycle is an unknown quantity upon the Grand Canal, none besides Lens, the St. Louisan who lost his life in Armenia, having ever passed that way until Mrs. McIlrath and myself appeared. The "devil carriages," as they called our wheels, were too much for their nerves to bear. Six miles up the Grand Canal we encountered the first village, and as the tow path ceased, and the only route through was by the main street, our speed was checked and we were prepared for the reception by the mob which we knew would turn up. By repeated cries of warning I kept the passage clear in front, but no sooner had Mrs. McIlrath passed than the mob closed in. Hooting and jeering, they followed at our heels, the larger and heavier knocking down and walking over the weaker and younger. Their discordant howls were deafening, and when the end of the village street finally appeared I signaled Mrs. McIlrath for a sprint, and away we sped, with a shower of clods after us. We traveled for thirty or forty miles along the banks of the canal, passing boats under sail, the crews of which shouted as we rolled along, until at last we sighted the south gate of Chang Chow, about 5 o'clock in the afternoon. Selecting a place where we could be protected from the wind, we stacked our wheels and prepared for lunch. A small spirit lamp boiled the muddy water taken from the canal. We filtered this through a little pocket contrivance and made each a cup of beef tea. We had expected to avoid being bothered by curious natives, stopping, where we did, one mile from the city, but before we had finished eating a dozen coolies and as many boys gathered around us, and with signs attempted to ascertain who we were and where we were from. Each boat that passed us hailed us cordially, but it was not until four hours after that a boat containing a party of missionaries, friends of ours, arrived, and we were taken on board and put away for the night. House-boats in China, where obtainable, are always preferable to inns, and it is well for one touring the country to attempt arriving at the water's edge by dusk.

After a good breakfast the next morning and a thorough inspection of our wheels, we bade farewell to our friends on the boat and set out for Ching Kiang. The streets in Chang Chow were very fair, and we made good speed through the city. Our appearance created a great commotion, but many of the crowd who clattered after us had heard of our reception by various notables and mandarins, and they saluted respectfully, at the same time assisting in clearing a way for us. Once on the open, we sighted the telegraph poles, and by following in their direction were soon on the Grand Canal once more. By noon we had covered forty miles, pausing for dinner at a small village. As we sat in the dingy, queer-smelling restaurant the sky darkened and rain began to fall. We saw the possibility of reaching Tan Yan before night growing less with each drop of moisture, but as the water did not fall in quantities sufficient to make the clay path treacherous, we mounted our wheels, determined to cover every mile we could before the downpour came. At 3 o'clock we sighted a high wall, which we knew to be that encircling the city of Pen In. We made no stop in the city, pedaling around the town, having been warned not to venture within its limits. We traveled all afternoon in a drizzle, and when the rain began to fall in sheets, about 5 o'clock, we were lucky in having a boat pass us on the canal. We hailed the craft, and by displaying a silver dollar obtained shelter for the night.

The following morning, Saturday, March 21, we again mounted our wheels and took to the tow-path. Though the ground was soft and treacherous, we reached

Tan Yan at 10 o'clock. It was amusing to observe the effect of our bicycles upon the natives. Farmers and laborers in the fields dropped their implements soon as they sighted us and ran to the roadside to view us in blank amazement, but if I stopped and attempted to engage them in conversation they directly ran for the interior again. Some of the people we passed with wheelbarrows left the vehicles in the path and sought refuge in the rice fields. A steam street roller could not have created greater consternation among a troop of wild ponies than our innocent rubber-tired vehicles did among the country folk of China. Several times we thought we had lost our way, so obscure had the path become, and had it not been for our compass, the knowledge that Ching Kiang lay directly north, and an occasional friendly farmer, we would never have found our way. Seventeen miles from Tan Yan we sighted the pagoda of the south gate of Ching Kiang, and entering upon a stone-bedded road, we plowed along at lively speed to the very entrance of the city wall. Inquiry for "Yen Isweesun" (foreigners) put to the crowd before us was fruitful, and under the escort of half a dozen young men we were led through a maze of small streets, and the way pointed out to a group of small houses which dotted the summits of a chain of hills. The United States flag floated over one residence, and with thanks to our guides we turned to leave them. The Chinese who had piloted us blocked our path, demanding a reward. By gestures they made it known that they would consider the account settled if I would let one man ride my wheel. Nothing could have suited me better, and I surrendered it at once. Two men held the wheel while the third mounted it, and in less than a minute he had taken a plunge into a ditch of muddy water, changing his ambition to ride into one of disgust for the wheel and respectful admiration for myself.

The United States Consul, Gen. A. C. Jones, occupied one of the handsomest houses in Ching Kiang. We called upon him on the afternoon of our arrival, but found him absent. However, we were taken into his office and entertained by Mrs. Jones until the arrival of her husband, who had been looked up by a native servant with the information that "two men" had come to see him "walking on wheels."

CHAPTER X.

GENERAL JONES ABLY REPRESENTS UNCLE SAM AND HIS GOVERNMENT—MUD DELAYS THE TOURISTS—MISTAKEN FOR A MISSIONARY M. D.

Gen. Jones, a tall, broad-shouldered man, whose handsome face was crowned with silvery white hair and ornamented by a flowing mustache and imperial, impressed me as one of the most courteous and affable gentlemen with whose acquaintance I had ever been honored. There are many reminiscences told of him and his admirable dealings in national affairs with the Chinese, and none better is related than how he adjusted the claim of his government arising out of the great riot of Ching Kiang in 1889. The riot, it may be remembered, resulted in the burning of the British Consulate, the looting of the American Consulate, and the death of Mrs. Mansfield, wife of Her Majesty's Consul, from shock and prostration. The claims of the British government were first presented to the Tao Tai, and after a long period of wrangling the amount of damages was considerably cut down and the matter was pigeon-holed for future consideration. When it came the American Consul's turn to present his bill, he did so without waste of words. It is told of him, by none other than Mr. Mansfield, the English Consul, that Gen. Jones disdained the seat offered him at the meeting of the Commissions of Arbitration, and remained standing in dramatic attitude before the Tao Tai. When that official had listened to the American claim, and expostulated that the figures seemed exorbitant, Gen. Jones drew himself up and forthwith gave an exhibition of Western ideas and American principles. Addressing the Tao Tai, he said:

"Sir, I represent a people whom your horde of fanatic savages have maliciously wronged and robbed. I have presented the claim; it lies before you. I do not ask that it be paid; I do not supplicate you that it be settled, but, as the representative of the United States Government, I demand, sir, that it be paid, unaltered, unchanged and in its entirety."

The Consul leaned over the table, one hand with clenched fist supporting his body, the other resting upon his hip, as if to draw a six-shooter, and with determination stamped upon his countenance, he hurled the words, rather than spoke them. The Tao Tai first appeared amazed, and finally he actually trembled with fear. The entire scene was theatrical, but the climax caused those assembled more astonishment still. After a hurried whispered conversation the Chinese officials nodded pleasantly to Gen. Jones, and the Consul took his seat. His claim had been accepted.

We had already been considerably delayed in our progress to Nanking, so charming and hospitable had been Gen. Jones and his wife, and, in spite of warm invitations to remain longer, Mrs. McIlrath and I left Ching Kiang at noon on March 22. Gen. Jones had ordered the way cleared for us, sending ahead a native officer. We had several days of hot, dusty riding, which was made all the more difficult by the increased amount of baggage which we carried. Nanking, our objective point, is the Southern capital of the empire, the home of the Kai King rebels; the site of the famous porcelain palace and of the great Confucian temple, a city which is the greatest of all Chinese educational points, as well as the most historical, offering opportunity for the examination of 28,000 students at one place at one time. Before entering the city we visited the Ming tomb, the burial place of the Emperor Hung Woo, who reigned during the fourteenth century, and dying at the Imperial Palace was interred at the foot of the Purple mountain. The tomb itself is simply a small hill, with nothing extraordinary appearing about its graceful, rolling eminence. Tradition has it, however, that in its depth reposes a magnificent vault, which has been completely covered by the faithful subjects who visited the tomb, each one depositing a handful of earth upon and about the vault. I bore a letter of introduction from one of my missionary friends to a Mr. Ferguson, an American resident of Nanking, through whose kind offices we were enabled to see nearly, if not all, the points of interest in the historical Chinese city, visiting the Bell tower, Drum tower and Examination Halls before our departure.

As Tai Ping Foo, our next stopping place, was 68 miles southwest, and over uncertain roads, we decided to remain the second night at the home of Mr. Ferguson, and it was not until March 23 that we took our leave. We were unable to get further than fifteen miles of Tai Ping Foo on account of the muddy roads. The clay collected by our tires blocked the opening in forks and frames, the sprockets were thick discs of the yellow, sticky mass, and every fifty feet we were compelled to scrape the mud off in order to move a wheel. Removing the chain from each wheel helped matters slightly, but so frequently did the cleaning process become necessary, that we no longer used a stick for the work, but simply scraped the mud from our tires and frames with our hands. Darkness overtook us and added to our discomfort. The path, only three feet wide, and built as an embankment, was as difficult to keep upon as a greased plank. Mrs. McIlrath and I fell time and again. Bridges had to be crossed on hands and knees, and so clogged with mud were our shoes that our legs ached from lifting our feet. We encountered many difficulties since leaving Chicago, but none so hopeless and with so little promise of a night's rest as the time we tried to make Tai Ping Foo. Mrs. McIlrath gave way to her feelings, and sat down upon one of the muddy embankments and indulged in a good cry. We wandered through the mud and rain the greater part of the night, plunging through rice fields and patches of mustard plants, guided only by the feeble light shed by our bicycle lamps. A bad fall broke the glass in my lantern, and we were then forced to proceed only by the dim rays cast by the lamp on Mrs. McIlrath's wheel. Toward morning we came to a halt in front of a mud hut, through the bamboo doors of which we could see the dying embers of a fire. I shouted several times before I could raise any of the occupants. A generous display of silver pieces persuaded them to let us enter. The wife arose, cooked us food, and made places for us to sleep on the floor, with the fire at our feet. I had expected my bill to be something enormous for this great accommodation, and I was all but stunned when our host demanded only 600 cash. This was equivalent to about 60 cents of Uncle Sam's money, which amount will keep a large Chinese family for a week. Tai Ping Foo by this time was only three miles away, and without further incident we reached the city, and though we had been awake the lesser part of the day, we were soon ready for another night's rest in more comfortable quarters.

A good stone road for seven miles rendered it possible for us to ride out of Tai Ping Foo the next morning, but by 10 o'clock we came again to the sea of mud, and were forced to resume our walk. We were successful in executing our plans to reach the river by dusk, for we had concluded to take no more chances in seeking shelter with the farmers. It was comparatively easy to obtain a boat to sleep on, and the yellow-skinned bandits took advantage of our position immediately. They seemed to realize just how badly we wanted a boat, and forthwith they put the price up to the excessive sum of four dollars. But boat we had to have, and I paid the sum, stipulating, however, that they were to carry us to Wuhu, seven miles distant, and land us by daybreak. For the only time in my dealings with these rascally natives they kept their word. When we waked we were in the midst of the shipping anchored about Wuhu. On shore I spied the Chinese imperial custom-house, and who should be stalking up and down the paved court before it but our English friend Burton, whom we had met in Shanghai! The meeting with him spoiled our plans for an immediate visit to Dr. E. H. Hart, surgeon of the American Methodist Hospital, as he introduced me to Mr. A. Knight Greyson, agent of the Jardine-Mattison Transportation Company. So genial was this hearty Britisher and his wife in their invitation to luncheon that we could not refuse, and in their cosy home, on the hulk of the old ship Madras, we ate the first good meal we had enjoyed for three days. Our letter of introduction was later presented to Dr. and Mrs. Hart, who not only received us with open arms, but placed fresh linen and clean clothes at our disposal.

It was necessary for us to remain three days in Wuhu. Our wheels needed a thorough cleaning, my correspondence had to be attended to, and our shoes and clothes were long past due for repairs. During our stay we were dined on board H. M. S. Daphne and the U. S. S. Detroit. Visits to us at Dr. Hart's from officers of the British gunboat, Commander Newell of the Detroit, Lieutenant-Commander Hawley, Lieutenants Evans and Desmukes, the British Consul, Mr. Mortimore, and the members of the various missions made time fly rapidly, and though the weather was most inclement, we were loathe to leave on April 11, when the sun at last showed himself. Hard riding, favored by delightful weather, brought us to Hankow within the week. My generosity in this part of the country turned out to be dangerous to the comfort of Mrs. McIlrath, as it almost exhausted my stock of medicines. We had stopped one Sunday on one of the boats moored in the river, and I was there mistaken for a doctor. The mistake was somewhat excusable, as Mrs. McIlrath, in a spirit of mischief, had told some of the fishermen that I was a "medicine man." I had taken a short walk on shore during the forenoon, and upon my return to the boat I found the "sick for the day" mustered in line along the beach. One child, suffering from what the missionary doctors call "rice stomach," or, in plainer English, indigestion, was the first to attract my attention. I sounded the little fellow's abdomen, which was so swollen that his waist girth exceeded his chest measure by fourteen inches, and prescribed and administered a dose for him. One of the sailor's wives was afflicted with the "cash eye," a poisoned and inflamed condition of the eye brought about by handling the dirty copper coin and then rubbing the eye with the contaminated fingers. The last of my patients was a young man who suffered from a toothache. I became on the spot a practicing dentist, cutting the gum away from the tooth with my pocket knife, and wrenching the offender from the poor chap's jaw with a pair of bladed pliers, which we carried in our repair kit.

At one of the villages we had passed before arriving at Hankow we fell in with a companion named Cunningham. His other name I do not remember, and it is just as well for his own sake that I do not, as I cannot help saying that Cunningham proved himself to be the most annoying part of our baggage. He was a good wheelman, but absolutely without "backbone," and in the serious encounters which we had with the natives, many of them being out-and-out fist fights, Cunningham proved the exception to the rule that Englishmen all are brave fellows and handy with their fists. He did the most injudicious things, and was directly responsible for several of our skirmishes. I may mention that we parted with him finally the day he chided Mrs. McIlrath for not coming to his assistance when he had been set upon and knocked down by a band of ruffianly coolies. Monday, May 18, 1896, I have down in my diary as one of the warmest I have ever passed through. The air was so humid and close that riding offered the only method of creating a breeze. The hot tea we drank at the villages did not alleviate our sufferings, and at my suggestion we passed the day in hard pedaling. Toward the evening we came upon a grove of gunbarrel trees, so called because the trunks are hollow like a gun barrel. The grove is situated upon the banks of a creek, and here we went into camp. The weather remained torrid, and for two days we rested in the forest. A settlement, not far distant, contained a market, at which we purchased our supplies, and the camping out was thus attended by much less inconvenience than one would imagine.

CHAPTER XI.

INTER OCEAN CYCLISTS ENCOUNTER AN ASIATIC SHYLOCK—
HAND-TO-HAND CONFLICTS WITH THE COOLIES IN
SHAZE.

On the eighth day of our trip from Hankow, Mrs. McIlrath contracted a severe cold, which impeded our progress and caused me great alarm. Much of the journey, on this account, had to be taken in sedan chairs. Our supply of tinned goods was also becoming low, the oil we carried for lubricating was gone, and Cunningham, as if to add his share to the chain of misfortune, displayed symptoms of malarial fever. As the only resort we changed our course in the interior and pushed toward the river, hoping to find some English steamer which might replenish our stores. A half day of waiting on the river bank, and a steamer hove in sight. The three of us hoisted signals, and I fired my pistols, but the steamer evidently did not see us, and steamed on up the river, displaying the English flag as she passed. Though not in such a serious predicament, our sensations were similar to those of the shipwrecked sailor adrift on his raft as the solitary ship sails by, majestic to look upon, but to the castaway cruel and cold. As if in sympathy with our disappointment, the rain came down in torrents as the steamer disappeared from view, and we made our way to a settlement a few miles ahead. It was then necessary for us to cross the river, which we did, but in the most unexpected fashion. The lone ferryman must have been an Asiatic descendant of Shylock, or at least his demands so indicated, for he asked 300 cash to row us 100 feet. To convey the impression that we were not in such a great hurry to be ferried, we sat down upon the river bank and began munching some tasteless cakes which Mrs. McIlrath had purchased at a restaurant. The large boat of a mandarin was moored upon the opposite bank, the crew watching us intently, and the official himself peering at us from the curtained window of his cabin. We next observed the anchor of the boat drawn up and the craft making headway in our direction. Just what was the mandarin's object in crossing we could not imagine. A plank was laid from the shore to his boat, and we were summoned on board. The silk-clad official received us politely, offering the customary tea. One of his crew, who knew a bit of English, interpreted to him that we desired to cross the river. In a moment our boat was moving, and we soon returned to the original mooring. It was almost too much to contemplate! For the first time we had been rescued from the exorbitant charges of a native by one of his own countrymen—a most unusual interference. Chinamen are very clannish, and seldom can they be induced to compete in prices when in trade among themselves, but never where a foreigner is concerned. Delaying only long enough to allow the mandarin to read my passports and to civilly refuse his invitation to remain on board his boat for the day and night, we landed and rode on our way.

Ten miles of very fair path through short grass brought us to a gigantic rock arising from the plain like a great castle. Under its sheltering shelves we found a trio of fisher huts. We stopped at the largest of these and obtained permission to cook the food which we purchased from the fishermen, one of the many luncheons of its kind that we ate in China. We stopped only long enough for our repast before setting out for You Chow. Before reaching the city we had a fierce hand-to-hand conflict with a number of savage coolies, Cunningham being almost annihilated. He brought it on himself, however, by rapping across the knuckles an inquisitive Mongolian who had dared to feel his bicycle tire. At You Chow we were received in great ceremony by the mandarin himself, who placed guards at our disposal, and offered us every protection, going so far as to volunteer sending men out to capture the natives who had assaulted us with clods and stones. The Tai Toa of the province visited us the next day to make changes in our passports. The Chinese map of China was produced, and by comparing it with the charts which we carried, I managed to show the official the route we had traveled since leaving Shanghai. One thing mystified me, I could not find You Chow on the native map, and after many efforts I succeeded in making myself understood. My breath was taken away when the official placed his finger upon the character indicating the city, and I learned for the first time that we were twelve miles from the Yang-Tse-Kiang and on the channel connecting with Tung Ting Lake. We had been lost the day before without knowing it. We had been in the dread province of Hunan, out of the territory permitted us to travel, and, worse than all, had put our heads into the lion's jaws by coming into the very place where lawbreakers are confined. I explained my position to the Tao Tai as well as I could, and he seemed to comprehend it. The next morning, Thursday, May 21, he had us called, gave us new passports for the province of Hunan, and dispatched an escort of coolies to see us safely started upon the right road. The issuing of the passport to foreigners by a Tao Tai, when not compelled to do so by a Consul, was unprecedented, and especially in our case, when he could have weighted us with chains, trussed us up like pigs to a pole, and had us carted overland to Shanghai. Such treatment has been accorded foreigners repeatedly.

It may seem strange to Europeans that the Chinese do not understand their own language when spoken by a native of some other province. Often in the short distance of twenty miles the dialect is entirely different. This fact I ascertained during our tour through Hupeh. The Shanghai resident is ignorant of the tongue of the Azecheun, and a Hupeh does not understand a syllable uttered by a native of Canton. The character used is the same when produced in writing, but the sound given it by the tongue is entirely different. Chinese also have the idea that natives from a distant province are not proper Chinamen. I asked a native of Hankow to interpret what a boatman was endeavoring in vain to say to me. My friend from Hankow made an effort, but gave it up in disgust.

"Can't you talk with your own people?" I asked, in amazement. "Can't you understand a Chinaman?"

"Chinaman," he retorted, sharply; "he no belong Chinaman; he belong Ning-poo-man."

And Ningpoo is one of the principal ports of China.

We had some difficulty and inconvenience in entering the city of Shaze, a city with a record of blood and crime unequaled to any in the Empire. Little of its importance is known to foreigners, or in the coast cities, although it is one of the most important towns on the river between Hankow and Chung King. Possibly this is because Shaze has not a bund, club house, race track, or any of the other modern "conveniences" of a large city. Only recently, or since the Japanese-Chinese war, had it been open as a treaty port, and during my visit there, two years ago, it had but one consulate, the Japanese. It was shunned by strangers on account of its reputation for being extremely anti-foreign, the ruins of a magnificent Roman Catholic Cathedral, standing like a specter on the river bank just above the city, testifying to this prejudice. The reputation of the place caused us to be extremely chary about entering, though we finally accomplished our aim under unlooked for conditions. The shore opposite Shaze was sparsely settled, and I was correct in my conjecture that we could obtain shelter in some hut across the river. The farmer who accommodated us was an unusually kind and intelligent Chinaman. We were kept as his guests three days by rain. On the third day I dispatched a messenger to the Japanese consul at Shaze, but the answer received, written in Japanese characters, occasioned me great disappointment. "No room for you; proceed on your journey," was the reply. I took this to be a Chinese trick, and accused the messenger of not visiting Shaze at all, but writing the characters himself. Later I learned that the letter had been taken to the Roman Catholic Mission by mistake. I returned the messenger to the city, and when he came back, an hour later, he was accompanied by a native, who brought me a letter which read:

> "May 26, Mr McIlrath, opposite Shaze, dear friends: We are received a letter with you and happy to say to you we are Christian Chinese and hope so are you. We have got good Chinese house in Shaze and hope you will come see us. And man will direct you to the right road to travel this side, and hope you will be happy to receive you. We are all Christians and hope so you are.
>
> Respectfully, S. Kwei."

The evident hospitality conveyed in the note caused us to overlook its ludicrous wording, and following without delay the "man," we reached the water's edge before we learned that he had failed to bring a house-boat with him. Directing him to return to his master, I gave him a second note, requesting that a craft be sent for us on the next day, and expressing our happiness at the prospect of visiting Mr. Kwei's house. By noon the next day the Inter Ocean tourists were comfortably fixed in a well-appointed Chinese residence in Shaze, the guest of Mr. Kwei. We were detained in Shaze until Saturday, May 30, and during the time that we were the guests of our host we were dressed in the gaudy raiment of the wealthy Chinese. When we left Shaze it was upon a large house-boat, bound five miles above the city.

The place scheduled for debarking appeared dangerous on account of the presence of a wild-eyed, chattering mob of coolies, and I prevailed upon the captain to take us further. We traveled over night, and early Sunday morning were landed at a point which promised fair riding. We were then upon our last relay of 300 miles. Ichang was our destination, and we estimated from the point at which the boat had landed us that we would arrive in that city by June 1. There were many annoyances and encounters on the road, some of them serious, as, for instance, a hay knife thrown at Mrs. McIlrath by a laborer in a wheat field. The weapon fell short, and was caught in the spoke of Cunningham's wheel. For the first time in our association did the little Englishman act promptly and correctly. He dismounted, and, picking up the hay knife, threw it far into the river. This act infuriated the Chinaman, who drew another knife, and calling to his friends, advanced toward us. To make a long story short, we "bluffed" the crowd with our pistols. The Chinese dread individuals who do not betray the rage they feel more than an entire regiment of blusterers. All of which reminds me of the well-known maxim that a "barking dog never bites."

When the Inter Ocean tourists reached Ichang they were half-way across China, with the record to their credit of 600 miles traveled through a country never penetrated by a foreigner before. Lenz, of whom I have previously spoken, followed the direct route from Shanghai, or what may be called the "telegraph line." Morrison and other Englishmen made the passage by steamer from Shanghai, and Stevens crossed only from Canton to Kui Kiang, and thence to Shanghai by steamer. It took us twenty-one days to complete the journey, and so anxious had members of the European colony at Ichang become about us that, had we not arrived when we did, native couriers would have been dispatched the next morning to search the country for us. Our first stop in the city was at the postoffice, where I received the note from Mr. Hunter, a friend we had met at Hankow, announcing that he had arranged for us to stop at the American Episcopal Mission, and that to the Rev. H. C. Collins would be due the courtesy of entertaining us. The first day we spent in Ichang thoroughly acquainted us with the members of the community. There were scarcely thirty foreigners in all, but each seemed anxious to render our stay as pleasant as possible. We had picnics, tennis parties and dinners arranged in our honor, meeting many interesting characters, both native and European. One of these friends, Tseo Shoo Wen, an energetic, lively Chinaman, and a man one could well afford to win as a friend, was especially solicitous regarding our comfort and safety. Learning that we were to travel through the Yang-Tse-Kiang gorges by boat as far as Wan Hsien, Mr. Tseo offered us as escort a gunboat and lifeboat. We declined, however, as we had been asked to become the guests on the house-boat of Dr. Collins, upon which we departed from Ichang on June 15. Our route as nearly as possible was to go by boat to Wan Shien, thence overland to Chung King, Suifoo, Yunnan Foo Tali and Bahme, the trip by boat merely allowing us to see the beginning of the beauty of the marvelous gorges, and not in the least rendering our trip any less interesting. In fact, as the summer floods were expected daily, there was greater hazard at this time of year on the waterways than on land. We were thoroughly stocked with bedding and canned provisions sufficient for a ten days' trip. We were so fortunate as to secure as captain the same native who had piloted one of my friends, Dr. Morrison, up the river, and he had retained his own crew of five strong, competent boatmen. The evening prior to our departure a complimentary dinner was given in honor of Mrs. McIlrath, and on Monday, June 15, the "Defender," as we called our boat, hoisted sail, and the Inter Ocean tourists left Ichang as they entered it, flying under the beautiful colors of the United States.

CHAPTER XII.

The rain which we had looked for did not disappoint us. The water poured steadily for three days following the Fourth of July, and on the 7th the water rose twenty feet in eighteen hours. It continued rising to flood height, and we were imprisoned at Ping Shan Pa until July 26, our boat tied to the trees of an orange grove which sheltered a coffin shop kept by an old man. The Yang-Tse-Kiang was in its fiercest mood, and none better than ourselves were in a position to witness its terrors. Our boat was turned and twisted as if struggling to break its bonds. Great volumes of under-current burst in swirls under our bow and stern, pounding as they struck the flat bottom of the boat as if we had been crashed on a submerged rock. The yellow waters seemed to leap in their course, all semblance to a stream being lost. Trees, torn up by their roots, leaped full length from the whirlpools and were drawn down into the vortex of the next. A capsized junk shot past, and as it was near the shore a half-dozen boatmen left the bank to seize the prize. It was an exciting sight. The crews raved, yelled and stamped on the deck like demons, risking their lives for the sake of a few pieces of silver. When they succeeded in beaching the junk, every plank, nail, bit of cargo, and even the bodies on board, were theirs to possess or claim reward for. The rampage of the river gave the coffin shop proprietor several days of grewsome work. Within twenty-four hours the gray-queued old fellow rescued six bodies from the whirlpools in front of his establishment. His son, stationed on a crag half a mile upstream, kept a keen lookout for the dead in the river, and as soon as the yellow, bloated bodies appeared on the surface of the water, he signaled his father, who, with an assistant, put out in a small boat to tow the corpses ashore. For this service and for the coffin he received 75 gold cents a body, and rich, in a Chinaman's eyes, had the old fellow grown with his years of watching during the spring and summer floods.

Ascending the gorges of the Yang-Tse-Kiang by boat is a trip which, under the most propitious circumstances, is fraught with danger and inconvenience, but especially so during the months of July and August. But we ascended the most dangerous parts of the famed canyons, passed through the Tan Hsin, Sung Poa Tso Tan and other dreaded rapids. Though the trip proved at all times exciting, there was no time that danger was sufficiently apparent to cause Mrs. McIlrath to change color or to reach out for her cork life-belt. Nevertheless, I would not undertake the journey again were it to lead through scenery doubly grand and were the passage to be paid handsomely in gold. The entire pleasure is lost in efforts to keep the Chinese crew in marching order, and, as they must be coerced into activity, the journey may be said to resemble an outing in the Grand Canyon with a herd of swine to drive. The expression is homely, but just and fitting. We sighted the beautiful Teng Hsiang gorge on Aug. 8, but long before we entered it the country became hilly, often resembling the beautiful Palisades of the Hudson. In America, where all things necessary to facilitate transportation and commerce are deemed absolutely necessary, such feats as the Port Huron Canal and the removal of Hell Gate are accepted by the public when the feats are accomplished as simply the result of need, but in China a mere passage a few miles long, blasted out of a mountain side, is a rare spectacle to behold. As our boat slipped along the rocks the beauty of the gorge disclosed itself, but to my mind the scenery of the Teng Hsiang gorge did not compare in grandeur to that encountered upon the rapids of Shan-Tou-Ping. The rapids are caused by jutting shells of rock running out into the river several hundred feet. As the water is deep, and the current runs eight miles an hour, the rapids are terrific. Had our boat broken loose and gone down stream onto the boulders, which reared their heads just above the water, boat, baggage, bicycles, and probably tourists would have been lost.

The mast of all boats ascending the Yang-Tse-Kiang is situated almost amidships, just a little forward, and to the base of this is fastened the tracking line of bamboo. From the top of the spar runs another line fastened to the towline about thirty feet out from the mast, and by pulling in or slacking this line the tracking line may be raised to the top of the spar, if desired, this to enable the towline to clear the rocks on the shore, which are occasionally as high as the mast. Forty coolies composed our crew on shore in charge of the tracking line, and as the "Defender," trembling and groaning, pushed her nose into the rushing water the crew ashore chanted and groaned, as, bent forward until one hand almost touched the ground, they moved us up stream. The night of our arrival in Kwei Chou Foo, an old and dilapidated, yet a city of great importance, Mrs. McIlrath and I slept on deck, as was our custom, awakened the next morning at daybreak. At 9 o'clock I sent my letter of introduction, card and passport to the Tai Foo by the captain of the lifeboat, and an hour later we received his card, and word that at noon an official would call for us. In the meantime our apartments were being prepared in the palace of the Tai Foo. He sent three chairs for us, one for myself, one for Mrs. McIlrath, and one for Leo, our Chinese interpreter, a Shanghai boy, who was quite driven out of his wits at the idea that one so high in rank should condescend to provide a chair for a foreigner's servant. The Tai Foo was a tall, slender man, middle-aged, and very intellectual in appearance. Beckoning us to a sumptuously furnished reception room, he welcomed us in courtly manner, and with Leo acting as interpreter, he asked the usual questions concerning our trip, the cause for undertaking such a journey, how much I received a month, if I had seen indications of gold and silver ore in China, and endless queries that are kept constantly on hand by the official clan. Gradually the potentate thawed out, his questioning ceased, and he began telling of his own affairs. He laid aside the peacock plumed bonnet and the gold breastplate, and, clad in his blue silk robe, he became simply a well-educated Chinese gentleman. He realized that Japan had annihilated and confiscated China's navy, defeated her troops and generally "played horse" with the Great Dragon. He also knew that the world was round, and that America and Great Britain were different countries.

We were the guests of the Tai Foo for three days, and when we were ready for departure he presented us with a purse of 20 taels, insisting that we accept it to remunerate us for the enjoyment he had derived from our honorable company. As a farewell contribution to our part of the entertainment, I rode the bicycle around the gardens, causing the wives, children and attachés of the Tai Foo to scream with delight, and then call for our chairs. As we took our places in the gaily papered interior of the sedans, the Foo's secretary handed me three enormous envelopes covered with imposing seals and large characters. These were letters of commendation to the Shen at Yan Yang Hsien, where we arrived Monday, Aug. 17. There was another official reception for us, with the same pageant of chairs, umbrellas and ponies. We dined with the Shen, who also stocked our boat with dainty dishes, including hams, ducks, chickens, fish and a young pig. The quantity of food provided for us as a single meal would have fed six Americans for several days.

The contract I had made with the boatmen called for 21,000 cash, and stipulated that we were to be landed in Wan Hsien in twelve days. The cash had been paid the crew in advance, and as the ship had occupied twenty-three days, I had been liberal in granting the crew extra money, until 17,000 extra cash had been added to the sum. But upon our arrival at Wan Hsien the boatman demanded 7,000 cash more. I had learned from experience that argument with the coolie class did not pay, so when the demand was made I requested that the boatman accompany me to the Shen and allow that official to decide the difficulty. This proposition he accepted, and as soon as we had met the official, presented our passports and letters of introduction, and our boy Leo had handed the Shen my receipts, contract and a statement of the extras paid, we adjourned to the trial room. In vain did our boat captain explain his woes as he knelt upon the stone floor. Unfortunately for himself, he attempted to explain some particular point, and instantly the Shen shouted an order, four coolies seized him, and stretching him upon the floor, administered 400 strokes with a club. I had not expected such an outcome, and when the Shen asked through the interpreter if I was satisfied, I could but answer, "Only too well." The boatman staggered to his feet, and with piteous moans was thrust into a bamboo cage. This seemed to be carrying things a little too far, and expostulating with the Shen I succeeded in having him released. Paying him 4,000 cash as a recompense, I sent him away, grateful that I had not taken advantage of my influence and allowed him to remain in the filthy bamboo pen.

The road from Wan Hsien to Chung King lies directly over the mountains. Knowing that upon our journey we would be unable to ride our bicycles, we engaged coolies to carry them, and taking the conveyance called mountain chairs for the accommodation of ourselves and boy, we left Wan Hsien Aug. 26. The Shen furnished us as an escort two soldiers and four extra coolies, and with these added to our party of five we made quite a little procession as we started on our long tramp. At 4:30 o'clock in the afternoon we halted at a large village thirty miles up the mountain. The rain was pouring, and while the coolies prepared a room for us in the inn I hastened to provide dry clothing and medicine for Mrs. McIlrath.

She had fallen ill during the morning, and had I known what distress and alarm her indisposition was to cause me I hardly think I should have ever ventured into the interior of China. To be ill in a civilized land, where one has all the advantages of medicine, proper food, bedding and pure air, is trying enough to one's nerves and peace of mind, but to be stricken in a land 300 miles from a white face, confined in a dark, damp room, centipedes crawling along the walls, rain dropping from the roof, terrible odors from pig pens in the next room, and cesspools of filth in the rear, is calculated to affect any sufferer for the worse. It was midnight before I could quiet my wife by the use of drugs. She insisted upon starting with us the next morning, though so weak she had to be carried to her chair. The rain fell in torrents, and to protect my patient I tied sheets of oil paper over her chair, wrapped her in a flannel blanket, and hung curtains of burlap over the doorway. Her condition did not improve for the next three days. The rain continued to add to our misery and discomfort, but my stock of medicine was running low, and I considered necessary a forced march to Chung King. Several times our coolie chair bearers mutinied, and upon one particular rainy night they gave us the slip, forcing me to send the Shen's two soldiers after them. They not only deserted, but took with them the chair used in carrying Mrs. McIlrath. But the soldiers were faithful to the friends of their master, and captured and brought back the truants. It was only by threats to do them bodily harm that I succeeded in making them resume the march next morning. I probably threatened more than I would execute, but prompt action was imperative. It was either to move rapidly toward Chung King, or lose by an agonizing death the little companion of my travels and of my life. The path was miserable, the rain fell in a drizzle, and the country was half hidden in banks of fog, but never did blue skies, green grass, and the sweet air of freedom appear more welcome to a released convict than did that dreary view as we set forward for relief.

CHAPTER XIII.

DESERTED BY MUTINOUS COOLIES—DANGEROUS JOURNEY
AFOOT TO CHUNG KING—THE MOST MYSTIFYING CON-
JURER OF THEM ALL.

Once well under way, our rebellious gang traveled peaceably, making good time, possibly because we would not permit them to stop for rest or a few whiffs of opium in any of the larger villages, thus frustrating all attempts they would be certain to make in endeavoring to enlist the sympathy of their fellows. The miserable gang, however, went upon another strike when at dusk we halted in the village of Huei Sung Chang. The village inn was dirty, as usual, and no more a fit place for an invalid than any of the other wretched quarters we had previously occupied. When we awoke in the morning of Aug. 31, Leo apprised us of the fact that rebellion had once more broken loose. The coolies refused emphatically to proceed without more cash. The first excuse was that they wanted food, but we had furnished that; the second they wanted opium, but the soldiers supplied them; the third, they wanted rice wine, and they had been given that also; and now they demanded cash. Nothing would satisfy them but good, copper hard cash. The soldiers threatened and argued in vain. The coolies knew that I had none of the little copper coins with me, my funds consisting only of large silver pieces. Their demand for cash was working both ways. If I did not give it them they had an excuse for leaving. If I did give it them they were just that much more ahead. I was about to repeat the object lesson of the day before when the boy Leo offered a solution to the difficulty by volunteering to proceed to the next city on foot, a distance of twenty-five miles, and exchange one of my silver pieces for the required coin. I accepted the proposition, and at 7 o'clock the next morning the faithful little fellow arrived with 5,000 cash. Two thousand cash were given the coolie gang and I demanded a completion of the journey and met with refusal. A squabble ensued and then the storm broke. About thirty coolies assembled in the front part of the inn and more filled the streets. With the aid of the one coolie, upon whom I could depend, I brought out our bicycles and luggage, lifted Mrs. McIlrath in my arms and placed her in the vehicle. This action was the draught of wind which fanned the spark into a flame. My own men took their positions silently and the little procession started through the long lines of humanity. The natives cursed, gesticulated wildly, some striking at us, and others threateningly displaying clods and stones in their hands. One villainous-featured old man followed us, talking confidentially to our men and slipping some article into their hands. This overt act, carried on through the medium of the long flowing sleeves, aroused my suspicion, and at the first village I stopped the outfit and investigated. Illicit opium selling was the meaning of the old fellow's sly actions, and I could but submit and allow the gang to fill their little tin boxes with the low grade "dope" and push on.

I have never seen outside of hospitals and museums such looking creatures as my gang of coolies were, when stripped. They were attenuated to such a degree that they were nothing less than breathing skeletons. Opium was responsible for it all. Yet there are men who profess to have traveled in China who deny that opium is the curse that missionaries claim it to be. I am positive that such men are either Englishmen protecting the infamy of their own land, which is largely an exporter of the drug, or else the remarks are made by men who frequent only the hotels and clubs at Shanghai, Hong Kong, Canton and Pekin, writing letters concerning a people the true character of whom it is as impossible to learn at any open port as it is to learn of Mormons, Indians or Indiana White Caps in Chicago or New York City. I have seen the opium fiend in all stages, from the novice to the exhausted hulk, who, paralyzed in every nerve, sits gaunt in a temple doorway, his sightless eyes staring with fixed glare from deep, dark-circled sockets. Every rib, every bone, even to those in his feet, could be seen, and were it not for the odor of the drug which permeates every fibre of clothing, they might be considered starved to death. Starvation really is the cause, for the devotee has no appetite only for the poppy drug. We employed coolies to carry burdens for us, who, in traveling one hundred miles, consumed only two bowls of rice during the four days spent in negotiating the distance. The rice and tea accompanying it cost 48 cash. The remainder of their wages, which amounted to 800 cash, was expended in opium. We have experienced the annoyance of waiting a half hour for men who had been smoking for four. Boatmen on the river, and laborers in the cities do not show the ravages of the drug as a class, for as soon as they become actual fiends they disappear from the busy arteries of commerce, just as drunkards do from active business circles in other lands.

MR. AND MRS. McILRATH AT CHUNG KING. — (See Page 58.)

There is a belt existing for a distance of 600 miles along the lower end of the Yang-Tse-Kiang where, at certain seasons of the year, principally September, October and November, the sun never shines, and if rain inaugurates the initial month a daily precipitation may be counted upon. We were in the center of this belt Sept. 3, and our own experiences gave evidence to the phenomenon. It rained steadily since our departure from Wan Shen, Aug. 26, and when we resumed our journey on Sept. 3, the roads and bridges rendered testimony to the effect of constantly rushing waters. Journeying under such conditions was not alone dangerous, but monotonous. One of the happiest moments of our tour was when we ascertained that Chung King was but little more than a hundred miles away. Several days drearily spent in climbing hills, wading small streams and skating through mud ankle deep, brought us within about five miles of Tu To. There we were met by a detachment of soldiers from Chung King. We learned from them that they had been dispatched by the Shen of Chung King to escort us to the city. We had lost so much time through bad roads and inclement weather that the officials of Chung King, who had been notified of our coming, had grown anxious and had sent out troops to guide us in safety. On Monday, Sept. 7, we obtained an early start, reaching a small village on the Yang-Tse-Kiang by noon. In small boats we embarked for the city, half a dozen miles above and across the river, arriving at 3 o'clock at the metropolis of Western China, a city situated on a point of land formed by the junction of the Yang-Tse-Kiang and Min rivers. Though Chung King has a greater population of foreigners than any other city on the river, excepting Hankow, we were astonished, upon arrival, to pass through miles of business streets without a glimpse of settlements of foreign houses.

It took much diligent inquiry for us to find the residence of Dr. J. H. McCartney, surgeon in charge of the American Methodist Hospital. We were a dirty, mud-stained pair when we at last ascended to the veranda of the doctor's comfortable home, but the kindly surgeon had heard of the Inter Ocean's enterprise, and he bade us enter before inspecting our condition. It would have made little difference had we been two-fold more dilapidated in appearance, for I never met a missionary surgeon in China who did not entertain us royally, even at the sacrifice of his own comfort. As he sat over dessert, discussing our journey, tasting the first genuine American pie we had eaten since leaving San Francisco, I learned with strangely mixed feelings that the district we had just traveled was the most dangerous in China. Only a few weeks prior to our arrival the imperial mail, carried overland, was robbed. I could then understand the significance expressed in the remark of a certain Shen when he said, "You will have plenty to cause you fear before reaching Chung King." I had told him that Mrs. McIlrath and I had no misgivings as to the trip, but had I known that mail carriers were assassinated monthly, and that commissioners, traveling under protection of one of the great power's flags, were robbed and maltreated, our answer would have been different.

The interior cities of the Chinese Empire are similar in every respect; see one of them and you have seen them all. A visitor to Ngau-King need not go to Shaze, the man who has seen Shaze need not travel in search of fresh sights to Chung King, and one who has seen the native city of Shanghai has literally seen the great aggregation. Chung King, situated 160 miles from the sea, differed only from the others in that the shops of the various trades were grouped, each industry occupying a section of the street. The only absolutely new features of the town appeared to be the climate, which is delightful for duck and pneumonia propagation, an old conjurer, and the industries established by Mr. Archibald Little. The climate is first and most important, since it exists in humid, opaque quantities upon all occasions, except perhaps when the sun does not happen to be busy elsewhere; then only does the sun shine in Chung King. Pig bristles are the fundamental property of the establishment of Mr. Little, and Uncle Sam's people are the chief patrons of it. After the porker has been despoiled of his hirsute trimmings, the bristles, sorted into bunches of three, four and five inch lengths, are wrapped and shipped to the United States for use in brushes. The remaining great attraction of Chung King, namely, the conjurer, we met on one of the quadrangles of a temple, and for a performance conducted in the open air, by a necromancer stripped from waist to crown of head, without apparatus or appliance, he was marvelous. In a circle formed by the crowd, the stone pavement serving as table and stage, the scrawny, wrinkled old magician produced from space a curved sword, iron rings, hardwood balls, clam shells and bowls. The performance opened with contortions of the legs and back, and a dislocation and replacement of the various joints of the body. The wizard then swallowed a hardwood ball two inches in diameter, following this with a few clam shells and poking the whole mass down his elastic gullet with a curved sword. Famous sword swallowers of the vaudeville stage of our own country may use longer instruments, and swallow equally large objects, but they always leave enough of the swallowed article outside their internal grottos to withdraw the obstruction. Our Chinese entertainer disdained these sensible precautions, and after we had felt through the abdominal walls the point of the curved sword, the ball and the clam shells, he removed them in a style which was distinctively all his own. To remove the sword, he contracted his waist by pressure of both hands, gave a convulsive upheaval and the weapon glided upward until just an inch or two remained in the throat. Then one of the spectators removed the blade at the conjurer's request. The clam shells and ball were brought to light in a simple manner, the conjurer not touching his hands to his mouth, but spitting them on the ground as soon as they appeared between his teeth.

CHAPTER XIV.

NEARING THE BOUNDARY LINE OF CHINA—A LONG TRAMP
WITH THE WHEELS AS IDLERS—A WARNING TO BANDITS.

We remained under the hospitable roof of Dr. McCartney's residence for nine days, during which time Mrs. McIlrath recovered from the serious illness which threatened her in the mountains. Her recovery dated from the moment we became the guests of the kind-hearted doctor, and was so rapid that she was able to attend dinner parties given by Commissioner Schutt, the Misses Galloway and Meyer, of the Methodist Deaconess' Home, Rev. Mr. Peet and wife, Rev. Mr. Mandy and wife, and to accept the invitation of the latter to visit their Industrial School two and a half miles from the city. As all these, except the commissioner, were from America, the time passed only too rapidly. The evening before our departure, we were very agreeably entertained by the Rev. Mr. and Mrs. Claxton, of the English Mission. We left Chung King Sept. 17, under Dr. McCartney's guidance, wheeling out of the west gate of the city. The sun had shown his presence on but one occasion of our nine days' sojourn, and our departure, like our entry, was made in a drizzling rain. Our road lay over hills and valleys through a fertile, but badly torn up country. Bicycling was out of the question and we carried our wheels slung on bamboo poles in such a manner that they would be ready for use in less than two minutes. To prevent rusting we daubed the nickeled parts and bearings with vaseline. The saddles were kept dry by tying oiled paper over the leather pads. Swung between the poles, which were carried by two coolies, the machines rode easily, and yet did not hamper the progress of the carriers. The luggage cases, with fresh white lettering, informed passers-by (or those of them who could read English) that the little procession of which the wheels formed the most interesting part, were on a "World's tour for the Inter Ocean, Chicago, U. S. A." We accomplished on an average forty miles a day until Sept. 20, when the signs of the country indicated that we were then in the last province of China, Yunnan, whose chief fame is in its proximity to Burmah. Great numbers of Mohammedans offering for sale beef, mutton and pork, were to be seen along the road. They were not in such number, however, that we felt encouraged in buying the flesh displayed, as the Buddhists were in great evidence, and being vegetarians, they never tasted meat. We therefore refrained from purchasing, reasoning that the beef was probably "shop worn."

The rain continued to fall in torrents and the last miles of our journey through China were made in an ocean of mud. Every garment we wore was soaked, our blankets wet through and through, and our shoes were in shreds. We had great difficulty in obtaining coolies to carry our burdens, and as I look back upon it now, I can scarcely blame them for not wishing to push on from early morn till night with a strong west wind driving the sheets of water in their faces. What the brave Lenz must have endured with no companion, I can well imagine from the recollections of the terrible mental depression offered by our trip. As Mrs. McIlrath and I trudged along, our very misery at times became so great that we were able to extract a certain hysterical amusement from it. My attire was conglomerate. A bicycle cap adorned my head; a Norfolk jacket my body; a pair of pajamas my legs; top boots over my feet, and straw sandals tied on these. Over my shoulders was draped my red blanket; on my back was strapped a Chinese sword; in my hand was a heavy walking-stick, and in my holsters a pair of rusty 45's. This mixture of bicycle, bedroom, Navajo Indian, cowboy and Broadway costumes delighted Mrs. McIlrath, who seemed to forget that she wore a dilapidated bloomer costume, patched half and half, with a man's sun helmet upon her head. Many of the temples, bridges and arches that we passed in the province seemed familiar owing to the photographs taken by Lenz and reproduced in his articles. I was much disappointed that I could not duplicate many of them, but the weather we encountered put an end to all thoughts of photography. Still tramping onward in the rain, the bicycles seemed to realize our misery, and occasionally when the wheels touched against some object they spun for minutes as if remonstrating against being carried and demanding an opportunity to "stretch their spokes." Careful inspection daily failed to reveal a fault or a flaw in the machines. Cyclists will be pleased to know that wooden rims stand all manner of climates. Since leaving Chicago in April of '95 to the September of '96, we had no occasion to alter or adjust either our rims or spokes.

On Sept. 24 we once more came upon the banks of the Yang-Tse-Kiang crossing and re-crossing it three times before getting to Sui Foo. In this part of the country we obtained our first view of a typical Chinese grove of feathery bamboo. Many writers have described vividly these beautiful pictures, but I fear many received their inspiration from a single tree scattered somewhere along the route of their journey. At any rate, I know that the bamboo flourishes in groves peculiar to this part of the empire, and I know further that, beside ourselves, Lenz and Margary have been the only ones who ever crossed China overland from coast to boundary line. General indisposition of Mrs. McIlrath, myself, and also of the boy Leo, delayed us at Sui Foo until Oct. 25. We wanted for nothing during our stop in the city, Dr. C. H. Finch and the Rev. Robert Wellwood of the American Baptist Mission being untiring in their attentions and courtesies bestowed. Our journey for the next few hundred miles continued to be one afoot. By the time we arrived at Poa Tung we were so road-bruised that we were compelled to knock off our journey and devote two entire days to the application of poultices and hot water to our swollen and blistered feet. On Sunday, Oct. 28, after a most exhausting tramp, the Inter Ocean tourists reached Tai Kwan Hseen. The road had been over the rockiest of mountain paths and we did not have an opportunity of riding our wheels until after we had passed through the cities of Chau Tung. More than one thousand miles of mud-plastered hills and half-submerged valley had we practically walked since entering Ichang, and more than 900 miles of that distance had been covered during rainstorms. Novice never was prouder, when discharged from the padded walls of a cyclery as a full-fledged rider, than were we as we flushed down a boulevard leading out of Chau Tung. We covered as much as fifty miles before a pause. In our enthusiasm we probably overlooked many defects in the road, and corrugations and boulders were passed over without any jar to the perfect contentment which rendered our spirits oblivious to slight inconveniences. Our stop at Chau Tung registered 9,000 miles over the worst roads in America, the best in Japan, and the miserable frame-racking paths of China, and our wheels still rode as easily and were as rigid as the day we pedaled out Washington Boulevard in Chicago. The people ran through the fields to head us off, here with laughter and approval and again with mumbled threats of resentment at the invasion of their land by "the foreign devils on iron horses." Old men joined in the unique procession which followed us at times for more than three or four miles.

Knowing that we could wheel but a part of the distance ahead of us, we had sent our bicycle carriers to be overtaken on the road ahead. We overtook and passed our coolies at a point precisely suited to our needs. Checked suddenly by a rocky hill several miles in length, we were forced to dismount, deposit our bicycles by the roadside and walk on. We might be considered rash for leaving our machines unprotected in such a barbarous country, but we knew that no persons were on the road between ourselves and coolies, and travelers going in the opposite direction would not be met with until after reaching the Half-Way Station of the day's journey. This important place Mrs. McIlrath and I reached fully an hour before our wheels arrived, and thus had plenty of time to marvel why, in such a miserable village of ten tea huts conducted by a hundred ragged, filthy natives, a magnificent triple archway of granite should be erected. Not one of the natives whom we questioned was able to explain this problem of why 30,000 silver taels of the people's money had been so expended.

The coolies overtook us with our wheels and fairly level roads enabled us to ride the greater part of the distance to Jeang Di, the village selected as the stopping place for the night. The paths were now trails worn deep into the clay by pony caravans, often so narrow that the pedals of the machines would strike the sides alternately, and so deep that our handle-bars skimmed within a few inches of the earth's level. We overtook a number of caravans, enjoying many comical antics by the sturdy animals who did not appear to be pleased at their first sight of the bicycle. Pedaling along the crests of the mountain ranges was delightful. Strong breezes cooled the air, and though the sun shone brightly we did not suffer from the heat until we descended into Jeang Di, dropping in five miles over six thousand feet. In the city the air found no possibility of circulation, and overcome with the intense heat and the exertion of the day, Mrs. McIlrath was compelled to retire, while I, scarcely able to understand the strange dizziness and confused vision, staggered about as if drunk until nausea informed me we had narrowly escaped sunstroke. We were told that many native travelers suffered in the same manner, and when the descent is considered the change is almost as sudden as cold, rare air to stifling heat. Bicycling was out of the question next morning and we sent our coolies ahead while we resumed our trip on foot. Far up in the mountains, where the air had again turned cold and the winds were biting and raw, we passed one of the hermit widows of China, a peculiar class of fanatics, who in Buddhist belief are said to receive great merit in the veiled world. Her husband dying while the marriage festivities were being celebrated, the widow vowed never again to marry or participate in earthly pleasures. So high in the mountains she made her home and upon a pallet of filthy straw she slept by night and sat by day.

In collecting curios we endeavor to select such of interest as we could conveniently carry without additional cost, but in Yunnan Foo we inspected a natural curio that I would pay any sum could I have transported it to America. The coveted marvel was Chang, the Yunnan giant. He was a better specimen of giant than his illustrious namesake who once toured the United States to his great profit. When only fifteen years old this junior Chang carried on his enormous feet six feet of manhood, and later increased his height to seven feet nine inches and his weight to 340 pounds. He wears a No. 13 glove and requires No. 14 shoes. When the missionaries ushered into our presence this massive form I was too stunned to speak. Clad in the red uniform of the Chinese army, his head wrapped in a black turban, he towered above me until I felt that he could not possibly be human. Being six feet and a fraction in height myself, I am accustomed to look down, or at best on a level, into the faces of other people, but to be compelled to bend my head sharply back to look at this huge fellow's shoulders was a decidedly new experience. As we were riding the "Great Stone Road" from Yunnan Foo we passed eleven small cages hung on eleven dead trees. In each cage rested the head of a human being. The sight was not one to be described. On the ground about the trees were baskets, ropes and yokes which had been used in conveying the heads from the execution grounds. Not one of the natives who hastened past with bowed heads dared to touch with foot or hand these abandoned trophies. At the next village we were told that the heads were those of eleven bandits who robbed a silk shop in the village, murdering two men and one woman, and almost causing the death of the aged mother of their victims. Decapitation was the punishment awarded, and that passing thieves might be warned against similar fates, the bodies were buried and the heads hung up as object lessons.

CHAPTER XV.

THROUGH CHINA INTO BURMAH—ENTERTAINED LAVISH-
LY BY BRITISH OFFICERS IN MANDALAY AND MADE TO
BLUSH AT A "ZAT PWEI."

Days of intense heat reigned, and snow marked our progress through the Yunnan and Kwei Chan provinces. The snowstorm rivaled in force a Texas blizzard,
so exhausting our coolies that they refused to go further. We gave them from our
surplus store of clothing, and put upon their feet extra pairs of our thick woolen
socks, so earning their gratitude that they consented to proceed a few miles further, where we came upon a large hut, which sometimes did service as a tavern.
We were snow-bound here for three days before we could push our way to the
British line.

Wednesday, Dec. 23, our last day in China, found us up bright and early, and
so impatient that we set out afoot in advance of our carriers. Up and down over
the stone-heaped path, passing numerous Chinese forts, and over three ranges of
mountains, we walked, climbed and stumbled until we sighted a more civilized
land—Burmah. Pausing only to assure our gladdened hearts that our eyes did not
deceive us, we plunged down a precipitous path, crossed a swaying suspension
bridge of bamboo, and, with a loud hurrah, landed on Burmese soil. Mrs. McIlrath's first action on the new territory was to flop down in the sand and cry; mine
to crack the neck from a small bottle, and, with a prayer of thanksgiving, a toast to
the United States, Queen Victoria, the Inter Ocean, and the good wheels we rode,
we drank the bottle's fizzing contents, and yelled like a pair of cowboys.

THE McILRATHS AT BHAMO, BURMAH. — (See Page 67).

At the water's edge weels squatted a few of Great Britain's defenders—the black Sepoys of India. We toiled up the hill to the stockade above, and as we approached, an individual, who introduced himself as Gordon, opened the barrier gates and invited us to come inside. Our advent was expected, and other formalities of introduction were unnecessary. We remained the guests of Gordon over night, as our coolies, with the bicycles, did not arrive until after sundown.

As I looked back over the last eleven months, my recollections become almost kaleidoscopic in their variations. For eleven months we were the guests of the Mongolians, having them for companions both day and night; we had adopted their customs, ate, slept and journeyed with them for weeks isolated from a white face, and we felt on our arrival in Nampong that we were competent to judge as very few others the true character of the long-queued Orientals. Our trip from Shanghai had involved 4,200 miles of walking, riding and climbing. We had been pursued by howling mobs; we had slept in swamps and rice fields; we had been fired upon, cut at with knives, lunged at by spears, and stoned innumerable times; often running a gauntlet of maddened natives, with clods and stones falling about us like hail. Coolies of the lowest and officials of the highest type had sheltered and entertained us; pleasures and pain had been our lot; from a palace as honored guests we had been altered in forty-eight hours to besieged beings, expecting to fight for our lives; lost in snowstorms, wading in streams, creeping around landslides, our journey has been fraught with many dangers; death in the garb of pestilent disease had brushed shoulders, feasted at the same table and slept in the same apartment with us; we had been ragged and hungry, yet now, on Burmese soil, not a word of regret could be expressed for all the hardships we had suffered. For myself, there is due little credit. I simply accomplished that which I understood must be done when we entered China, but to the heroic little woman who pleaded to be allowed to share my hardships, is all credit due. Never did she falter when the mobs gathered around us, and when the last possible recourse permitting escape from death and torture seemed exhausted, she was firm and quiet.

Of the Chinese as a people, individually and collectively, we learned them to be a weak race, morally and mentally. Opium, liquor and disease have set their marks upon millions. In trade the natives are unscrupulous, and chivalry or respect toward women does not exist. Cruel to the extreme, with a cultivated ferocity they are most arrant cowards, and yet, most overbearing when in numbers. The country itself is rich with precious metals, commercial minerals, oil and fibrous grasses, as yet either unknown to the natives, or else requiring too much labor to extract. Improvement or advancement in civilization or mercantile industries will never take place in China while governed by China. The supreme egotism of the natives prevents the adoption of anything modern or anything foreign. The official classes are no less corrupt. Banded together, as if a society for pillage, they prey upon the people, aided by the more unprincipled priests, and woe to the merchants and peasants who enter court to obtain justice. Such, briefly, is China as the Inter Ocean cyclists found it to be.

The first Burmese village into which we wheeled was Myathit, situated in one of the dustiest, hottest, driest portions of all India. There were fine shade trees dotting the white, dusty road, and everywhere were to be seen the curiously attired people from all parts of India and Burmah. I could distinguish the Indians by their garbs of white, some cut into long frock coats and tight trousers, others into jackets, with long, flowing trousers gathered at the ankles. Huge white turbans were knotted about the heads of the Indians, a bit of bright color in the center being the only relief in the entire study of black hands and faces framed in a setting of immaculate white. The Burmese women, as a rule, are handsome. I was aided in this discovery by Mrs. McIlrath, who pointed out to me, as a type, a beauty possessing a complexion like cream, with the pink tint of peach blossoms. When Mrs. McIlrath announces that a woman is beautiful I accept it without argument. She, and not I, is the censor in such matters.

One could not imagine a more insipid place to live in than Bahmo, the military and trading coast where we were quartered. The hours of life are routine and monotonous, excepting when one is fortunate enough to own a membership or to have a card to the Bahmo Club. For thirty days in luxuriant idleness (of course not counting the many short trips awheel in and about the city), we lingered in Bahmo, living in the bungalow of the China inland missionary. Bicycling in the district of Bahmo affords limited journeys, but we managed to travel twenty miles away, and visit the government hospital, the provincial jail and a number of coffee plantations.

We sailed from this large, but rather uninteresting, city on Jan. 25, 1897, taking passage on one of the Irrawaddy Flotilla Company's mail steamers, the Monein. After three days' steaming the Monein tied up at the dock in Mandalay, the capital city of Burmah, and sung of by Mr. Kipling in his clever verses, "On the Road to Mandalay." During the reign of Kings Mindoon and Theebaw, in order that the palaces might be protected from invaders, the buildings were erected far to the inland, under the shadow of Mandalay hill. Wheeling over the hard macadam was a delight, and merrily we whirled off the miles intervening, until we alighted, at last, at the European hotel, the first that had welcomed us since leaving Hankow, China. In our journey of the globe, having been the guests of thousands of people, we must credit the members of the Burmah Club, fifty per cent of whom are British officers, with being the most attentive and kindly organization at whose hands we received courtesies. As a body they wined us, dined us, gave picnic excursions on the river, drives, bicycle rides, obtained invitations to various native celebrations, and put forth every effort to render our sojourn instructive and pleasant. Bicycling with several Europeans who were fortunate enough to own cycles was one of the most delightful features of our entertainment. The roads were excellent, and wheeling in the cool air of early morning, one of the many delightful temples or majestic pagodas the objective point of our excursion, is a pleasure to be enjoyed only on British roads in an Oriental country. It was our privilege, on Feb. 12 to witness a wedding of royal blood. The ex-Nyanugwe Saw Bwa "requested the pleasure of the company of Mr. and Mrs. McIlrath at his home, in South Moat Road, on the occasion of the marriage of his daughter Saw Kin Gwi with the Saw-bued of South Theinni, and also on the same night, to witness a Zat Pwei." The ceremonies were performed by the highest class native officials and Sir Frederick Fryer, first lieutenant governor of Burmah. To appear successfully at such a state function one is supposed to dress appropriately, and I felt greatly embarrassed in my knickerbockers as I mingled in the blaze of red uniforms, royal Scotch plaids, gold lace, decorations, and the jewels and dainty gowns of the ladies. Extravagant as are the English in costuming for each event and occasion of the day, the guests did not appear to notice the greasy, dusty and patched raiment which comprised my only wardrobe, and did all they could to make me feel at home. The verbal portion of the marriage ceremony was unintelligible to me, but the "business," as an actor would describe it, made it quite plain to the most casual observer that the dusky pair who formed the center piece of a most interesting group were being united in the holy bonds of wedlock.

The usual check from "papa" was not seen as we inspected the wedding gifts, but there was a profusion of diamonds and silver plate. The diamonds were just such as are admired by Burmans, huge yellow beauties, set in dull gold rings, the base uppermost and the radiating surface concealed. Just why the Burmans reverse the European idea of setting gems is difficult to explain, but the prevailing idea is that the gem is so set to resemble the pagodas and pyramids so omnipresent and revered in Burmah. Diamonds valued as high as 30,000 rupees, or about $10,000 in our money, are set in this manner, and the color is invariably yellow. The Zat Pwei, which was next on the program, proved to be a theatrical performance. It began with an overture by the orchestra, the music typically Oriental; then came the dancers of the company, followed by the event of the evening, the drama. Just what the play was called, or what the plot was about, was vague to all the Europeans present, but as the dialogue progressed the audience warmed up and the actors became enlivened. Dropping their theatrical drawl and stagy manner which had characterized the first half hour, the performance developed into repartee of suggestive tone. In fact, the most unblushing French jokes would look well upon Sunday-school cards after listening to a series of Zat Pweis. As our party was entirely dependent upon a native interpreter for translation, and as this gentleman did not regard the performance from a European standpoint, the entertainment soon reached a stage which required the withdrawal of the ladies, and at midnight, with a farewell congratulation to our host, we returned to the hotel, satisfied that Zat Pweis were most interesting—to bachelors and a few other gentlemen.

CHAPTER XVI.

Cycling in Burmah proved extremely monotonous, and the dullest of all the dreary rides we experienced were here. Nowhere was there a variety of scene or change from the level valley, with its dusty, winding roads stretching out under the blistering tropical sun. The air was ever stifling hot; it smarted our dilated nostrils; seemed to stuff our gasping lungs and blister the backs of our hands and necks, and a ride of three hours at a stretch caused us to relax into a sort of stupor, from which we could only arouse ourselves by repeated efforts. Had we reached Burmah during the fall of the year, we could have made good progress, but now tedious delays, entirely beyond our control, hampered us, and we had to face not only the famine and plague-infested land, but the white man's greatest enemy, the summer sun, which, in its molten glare, kept the temperature above 100, night and day, making death and heat apoplexy quite as possible as from the epidemic of cholera and bubonic fever. We left Mandalay at daybreak on March 1, and started over the dusty roads to Rangoon, 400 miles south. Mandalay had been the point which we had selected to observe the characteristics and customs of the natives, and, unlike the efforts put forth in the same channel in China, we found the duties pleasant and fraught with happy little incidents. Burmans resemble the Japanese to a certain extent; not so cleanly, energetic, intelligent or independent, but possessing the same admirable faculty of being happy, smiling and self-complacent under circumstances which would fill any other being's soul with pessimistic vagaries. Farming, carpentry and carving appear to be the only occupations left them, for everywhere was seen the submissive black who followed the rush of England into the land of milk and honey and rice and rubies.

"Othello's occupation gone" is true of the Burman. Blacks are the scavengers, sweepers, table servants, cooks, butlers, porters, coachmen, tailors and merchants. Eurasians, the half-castes, whose yellow skin and coarse black hair betray their early English ancestors, and the blacks are selected to act as clerks, hospital attendants, telegraph operators and railroad clerks. "Baboo," the English and natives call them, and, if another letter had only been added to the name, the term would have been quite appropriate. With all these occupations lost to him, the native still appears to do well, always in silk and spotless muslin, smoking incessantly cigarettes or huge cheroots, which scatter sparks like a working fire engine. The women of the Indian races act as laundresses, nurses and maids. Thus, with almost all the natural trades and occupations taken by invaders, little is left for the Burman but the profession of thief and thief-catcher, both synonymous in Burmah, where a policeman is feared not for his authority, but for the blackmailing such office permits him to levy upon wrong-doers and innocent upon whom suspicion rests.

We had many companions on the road to Rangoon. On every side were Burmans on foot, on horse, and in the low-roofed box-like carts, which creaked and groaned as the gentle, curved-horned beasts drew them along. We passed Indians who walked hand-in-hand, and Chinese gardeners who swung along at a rapid pace, though their backs were bowed with the weight of fresh vegetables. Bicycles did not seem to attract much attention in the motley throng, the only persons acting as though our presence was unusual being the women bathing around the stone-topped wells, and they only because the icy waters that dashed and poured over their bodies had caused the only garment they wore, a short, scant skirt, to cling closely to their limbs, revealing every outline of symmetrical figures.

THE BICYCLE SURPRISES THE BURMANS.—(See Page 70.).

The craze for wheeling had just reached an interesting stage in Rangoon at the time of our visit. The demand for machines exceeded the supply, and as a result there was to be seen every morning and evening the most interesting parade of antiquities ever witnessed outside of a bicycle show. American machines of modern make were a close second to the new English product, but wheels entitled to the utmost respect due to old age formed the creaking, groaning majority. The riders, too, were curious, the Europeans first in numbers, Eurasians second, and the Indian-Chinese-Burman, the mongrel of all Asia, making up the balance. The positions, too, some of the riders assumed were remarkable. The "hump" had not reached the far East, the rat-trap pedal and toe-clip were unknown, and with handle-bars wide as the horns of a Texas steer, seats suspended on coil after coil of spring, low and set far back over the rear wheel, the tread eight and ten inches wide, the riders reversed the "hump" and appeared to be sitting on the dorsal vertebra, pumping much as a bather swimming on his back. There were many places of historical interest in and around Rangoon, and as all points were available by cycle, our good old wheels were kept busy. The turning point of our morning spins, the teak lumber yards, permitted sights which would delight the little folks at home as much as they secured the attention of tourists here. Elephants, great, huge, dirty fellows, void of all the tinsel trappings of the circus, were the attraction, as daily they performed the most arduous labor which in America is done by cranes and derricks. In harness of chains, the beasts drew enormous logs from the river to the carriage at the saws, and with ropes wound around their trunks they dragged the rough slabs into a yard and piled them in precise heaps. With trunk coiled as a cushion against their tusks, they pushed enormous pieces of timber into the proper places, each piece being placed in exact position, with the ends carefully "trimmed." Gentle and meek as the laborers are in appearance, as, with flapping ears and timid little eyes, they obey their commands, they sometimes become mutinous. In the McGregor yard, which we visited one morning, we were shown one of the largest and best workers of the herd, who had just been released from "jail." He had been in confinement four months, laden with chains, deprived of delicacies, and treated as a criminal, simply because he had wantonly walked upon and then tossed his keeper into the air. The beast apparently realized the disgrace which had been heaped upon him, for he obeyed his new master without even pausing to blow dust on his back or plaster his huge sides with cooling, fly-proof mud.

With the advent of English rule in Burmah, native athletic sport degenerated, and became supplanted in time by horse races of most corrupt nature. When I state that the racing is corrupt I have but to cite two instances which occurred at the meeting of the Mandalay Club during our visit to that city. A captain in Her Majesty's army placed 3,000 against 1,000 rupees that a certain horse, which we will designate as A, would win over the field presenting two horses, B and C. Of the latter, C was clearly outclassed, consequently the race was between A and B. You may judge of the bookmakers' surprise when they learned in the afternoon that the gallant captain was to ride B, the horse he had bet against. The race had but one possible outcome, A won. Another race was started and finished in absolute darkness. No lights were used on the tracks, the horses were dark in color, and the jockeys the same, but the judge readily named the winner, and the bookmakers lost again.

A native prize fight is even more remarkable, though always conducted "on the square." I do not know the rules governing the ring in Burmah, but so few methods of attack are barred that one need not bother himself on that point. Biting, hair-pulling and kicking a fallen opponent are the only prohibited acts. I was invited to be present at a series of combats which took place in the arena near the Shway Dagon pagoda in Rangoon. Facing each other, the fighters stood a pace apart, the referees opposite each other, also, forming a square. The referees clapped their chests, the combatants smote themselves likewise, there was a great roar of voices, and before I could really notice how it happened, the fighters were wriggling on the tanbark. A flash of dark skins through the sun's rays, the clapping sounds of palms on necks, backs and thighs, a catherine wheel of legs, arms, heads and tanbark, and the round was over. Separated by the referees, the men retired to their corners, drank bottles of soda water, took fresh chews of betel nut, and good-naturedly listened to the gratuitous advice from their friends in the audience. The referees called round two by slapping their chests. The fighters were more cautious as they went at each other, the up-country man opening the round by kicking his antagonist in the chest. A vicious uppercut with a swinging knee was next landed by the local man, and as it reached the curry and rice department of the up-country man, events looked bright for Rangoon. Blows, swung right and left, up and down, were delivered like a man chopping wood. The Rangoon man made a supreme effort to feint, and in doing so he actually struck something, and unexpectedly ended the bout. Leaping high in the air, he kicked the up-country man square on the nose. The blood flew, and the fight was over. Blood drawn, if only from a scratch, constitutes a victory for the unbled one, and two minutes later the fighters had received their reward, coins tossed into the ring by spectators.

Two years to a day after leaving Chicago we walked up the gang-plank of the steamship "Africa," booked for Calcutta, only three days across the formidable Bay of Bengal. Mrs. McIlrath developed her usual attack of sea sickness, though the water was unruffled, and was kept in her cabin for the entire voyage, leaving me to occupy the daylight hours wandering among the deck passengers. The first impression one receives on landing at the port of Calcutta is that the city is one vast cab stand. "Gharries," as the natives' hacks are called, line the walks, crowd the streets, rest under the shades of trees in parks, and stand at the curb in front of hotels and shops. The dust, rattle and bang caused by these shaky, dirty vehicles, which are dragged about by horses at snail's pace, is a nuisance second only to the tram cars, and one which would be tolerated only by custom-bound, "strictly-in-form" Englishmen. Streets in Calcutta wander aimlessly along, similar to the rail fences in Indiana, and the buildings, uniformly of staff-covered brick, are of every imaginable size and shape, as if architects were of one mind in determining to try all kinds in an effort to obtain one adapted to the climate. Sidewalks, roads and paths are packed with white-clad natives, barefooted and bareheaded, in the awful glare of heat, which strikes horses dead, unless their heads are protected, yet none of the blacks appear to suffer. Doors of hotels and shops are kept open, but hanging in the apertures are heavy mats of a peculiar grass, which coolies wet with pails of water, and by which means the air is cooled. Everywhere the heat is talked about and guarded against, and yet, with huge fans swung constantly over one's head, with cooling draughts on a table by your side, the perspiration pours from every part of the body. One hundred and ten degrees in the shady corridors of the Continental hotel, the coolest in all India, 98 degrees at night, and this was the country we crossed on bicycles, involving over 2,000 miles' travel, and beyond the pale of ice or daily clean clothes! Bicycles are ridden extensively in Calcutta, comparatively speaking more than 3,000 wheels being enumerated in the tax list at the time I was in the city. There are, however, only about three months in the year favorable to riding—December, January and February. In other months cycling is tolerable only between the hours of 5 and 8 in the morning and evening. This, of course, applies only to the Europeans, and not to the natives, who ride in the intense heat of midday without the slightest difficulty. A sight calculated to arouse laughter in a wooden cigar sign is one of the proud possessors of an old solid-tire, with hammock saddle and wide handle-bars, as he plows along the road, making erratic dives, like misbalanced kites.

The most frequented road is a short strip on the Maidan, an enormous clearing, five and seven-eighths miles in circumference, in which is situated Fort Williams. Roads of fine macadam skirt the park, and amid cricket, golf and football grounds are statues and columns erected to Englishmen who have performed satisfactory duties in India. Eden Garden, at one end of the Maidan, is a beautiful spot, and here, morning and evening, a well-directed band plays sweet music to charm Calcutta's conglomerated inhabitants. Cycling in early evening along the Strand is also gratifying. The street is crowded with women in white and red robes, silver anklets and bracelets, their head and matchless figures but faintly concealed by flimsy togs. Burning ghats are also erected on the river shore. The Calcutta burning ghats on the Strand road affords accommodation for the cremation of sixteen bodies simultaneously. In appearance, the crematory is unpretentious, simply a low-roofed structure divided into an alcove, and two waiting rooms for mourners. The Inter Ocean cyclists visited the crematory, and were shown throughout the establishment by an aged Hindoo, who superintended the force of men who kept going the coals under fifteen pyres. Not of less interest, but far less disagreeable, is a distinctively Calcutta feature. Kali ghat. This is a temple devoted to Kali, goddess of destruction, reputed in Hindoo lore to possess a thirst for blood, and to appease and propitiate whom live sacrifices are made. Formerly human beings were offered, but under British rule the custom was abolished, and kids and goats substituted. Decapitation is the method offered, and as fast as sacrifices are brought forward, the bleeding little things are seized by the ears, the priest makes a cutting slash with a heavy knife, and the headless trunk is thrown to the ground. We witnessed the religious rites of Japanese and Chinese, and we had seen the medicine-dances of the American Indians, but nothing approaches the furious fanaticism and the frenzy of the Hindoo at Kali ghat. Men shouted themselves hoarse, women screamed and tore each other's clothes at the shrine of the goddess. It took the assistance of half a dozen hired blacks to force for us an entrance into the temple, and rushes of worshipers were so great that thrice we were swept back ere we obtained a glimpse of the hideous deity. Her face and figure a blood red; with multiple arms swaying like the tentacles of an octopus; her face distorted with blood red tongues; a necklace of skulls about her throat, the goddess Kali is indeed the representation of destruction. Gross, hideous and repulsive as was the figure, the effect was heightened by the maddened crowd, who, with wild shrieks, tossed offerings of flowers at the fiendish idol in their effort to escape from the calamities, believed in their pagan minds, to be brought about by neglecting to satiate the goddess' greed for bloodshed and crime. Amid such surroundings it was not to be wondered at that our minds reverted to the fact that "ghazi," the assassination of Christians, is still in vogue in India, and that one of the devout worshipers might easily plunge a knife in our backs, and thus earn his way to Hindoo heaven with ease and glory. I can assure my readers that we felt easier and more comfortable when once more in our gharry and the horses on a dead run en route back to the hotel. We learned from a priest at the ghat why Calcutta is so named, the title being a British corruption of Kalikata, the name bestowed by the Emperor Akbar, in 1596, in commemoration of the proximity of Kali ghat. We were in Calcutta two weeks before the cycling fraternity knew of our arrival. When they finally discovered our presence, we floated along on a wave of popularity. Cyclists, dealers and agents were our daily companions and callers. American machines were well-known and liked, and wood rims and single-tube tires were looked upon with doubt, but after an inspection of the hardest-used pair of wheels the world ever knew, wood rims and single tubes took on the ascendency.

CHAPTER XVII.

NIGHT RIDING THROUGH INDIA TO ESCAPE THE HEAT—
THREE IMPUDENT ENGLISH WHEELMEN ENCOUNTERED
AT BENARES.

We left Calcutta early on the morning of May 4, taking the Strand road, across the sacred Hoogly river by means of the Jubilee bridge. We were accompanied for a brief distance by Mr. W. S. Burke, editor of the Asian, the only legitimate sporting paper in the East. To this gentleman were the Inter Ocean tourists indebted for maps, guidance and excellent entertainment while in the city. He piloted us through a road shaded by magnificent palm trees, an avenue 40 feet wide, level as a billiard table and smooth as asphalt. Mr. Burke informed us that this was the "Grand Trunk" road, our path across India from shore to shore. Most of our riding was done at a fast clip, in spite of the fact that we carried full luggage cases, camera, guns, water canteens, lamps, and bells to the extent of 50 pounds each. Only twice did we dismount in the twenty-five-mile run to Chandernagore, once to induce a cautious gate tender at a railroad crossing to open the gates, the second time to view the terrible cars of Juggernaut. Much has been written concerning these vehicles and the manner in which they are hauled about on festive occasions, and in former days crushed out the lives of hundreds of devout fanatics, who endeavored to reach heaven by self-sacrifice. One would naturally believe that such barbaric practice had been done away with by British rule, but such is not the case, and, despite the presence of police and soldiery, each time the towering car is hauled out by worshipers some poor, weak-minded wretch hurls himself under the ponderous wooden rollers.

"As the cycle lamp's rays penetrated the gloom they revealed a large, fine cheetah, or panther, crouched in the edge of the brush, his eyes fixed on the glare of my lamp, his fangs disclosed in deadly array." (See Page 80).

Burke, good-natured, fat and jolly, left us at Chandernagore, but not before a breakfast at the same hotel where, three years ago, he had breakfasted with poor Lenz, served by the same woman, who spoke also of "the fine little lad" who was lost in Armenia. Intense heat made riding dangerous during the day, and after we left Burdwan, on May 5 (81 miles from Calcutta), the greater part of our progress was accomplished at night. We never realized what Indian heat signified until now. The coolness of night offers many inducements for bullock-cart caravans to travel, and a sharp outlook has to be maintained for these obstacles. Our arrival at the Hotel de Paris in Benares, on May 12, completed one-fourth the run across India, a total of 496 miles from Calcutta, representing a succession of night rides, with stops for refreshment and rest at the bungalows along the route. Night riding in India is the only way to avoid paralyzing heat, but it has its terrors and dangers, and after some of my experiences in the jungle between Delhi and Benares, I should say that if I had the trip to make over again, I should undoubtedly trust to the mercies of the sun. We encountered leopards by the score, and though leopards in India are not supposed to attack humans, we could not help our misgivings at the sight of the graceful creatures, as they silently bounded their way through the jungle.

Our arrival at the Hotel de Paris caused much excitement. The English do not read newspapers as generally as do the Americans, and, with but one exception, not one man around the hotel had the slightest idea who we were, where we were from, or what we were doing. In fact, after reading the "World's Tour for the Inter Ocean, Chicago, U. S. A.," as printed in large white letters on our luggage cases, many asked us politely, "Pray, what is the meaning of the legend?" We had learned while in Calcutta that Messrs. Lowe, Lum and Frazer, who had left England on a cycling tour of the world in 1896, were on their way across India, and that in all probability we would meet them in Benares. We looked forward with much pleasure to the occasion of joining hands with cyclists who understood the hardships of great journeys in strange lands, but the meeting occasioned us an unexpected set-back in our natural affection for fellow wheelmen. The trio arrived on the second day of our visit in Benares, and immediately sent word that they wanted to see me. I called upon them, and was greatly surprised to ascertain that they looked upon Mrs. McIlrath and myself as frauds. They questioned me closely as to my journey, and concluded by commenting upon the strangeness of the fact that they had never heard of us before. This I did not regard as unseeming, since few of the inhabitants of "the tight little isle" do know what is occurring in the greater part of the world not under British taxation. Fifteen minutes' conversation with the Frazer outfit convinced me that the new aspirants to globe-girdling honors entertained little respect for Americans in general, and ourselves in particular. Lenz they declared emphatically a nonentity in cycling history; Tom Stevens was totally unreliable, and as for ourselves, we had undergone no hardships, and were comparatively new. They probably did not like Stevens because he was the original "round the world on bicycles;" Lenz because he had accomplished single-handed more up to the time of his death than these fellows could accomplish over the route they had selected, if they completed their program; and Mrs. McIlrath came in for her share of contempt because a wee, slender woman, she had encompassed what they averred they would attempt, in a number strong enough to cross the threshold of any earthly inferno with impunity.

Their object in circling the world was simply to make the journey, selecting the shortest, most expeditious route, and arriving home as quickly as possible. Frazer was once a "journalist," he informed me, but had deserted journalism to become an author, and write stories for a magazine called the "Golden Penny." While I confessed knowledge to the existence of the Strand, Pall Mall and other magazines in England, I dropped another peg lower in the estimation of my friends because the "Golden Penny" was not included in my list of acquaintances. The machines the cyclists rode were, of course, English make, weighed twelve pounds more than our own, and were equipped with mud guards, gear cases and brakes. The tires were double-tube, and the fourth pair for each machine were now in use, while we were using the same set of single tubes placed on our wheels in America. Their machines showed signs of wear, the front forks of each having been broken, and now, after only one year's use, the frames creaked painfully and the apparatus generally looked badly "used up." The luggage of each man was carried in a small valise fastened on the mud guard over the rear wheel, and large tool bags hung in the angles of the frame. Each carried a short-barreled, cheap revolver, and Lowe, the most gentlemanly and intelligent of the trio, carried a camera. It is needless to comment further upon these gentlemen. They announced their intention of visiting America, and one declared, as I informed him how cordial he would find our cyclists, mayors, governors, and even the president: "We shall not bother about Americans much; after being entertained by the Shah of Persia, we have decided to let your American dignitaries alone."

We were entertained, while at Benares, in the castle at Fort Ramnagar by the Maharajah of Benares, one of the native princes of India. His Highness sent a magnificently appointed carriage to the hotel for us, with the proper quota of coachmen and liveried footmen; greeted us in excellent English, and soon displayed his foreign tendencies by direct inquiry about cycling, American foot-ball and baseball, proudly assuring us that he was an enthusiastic foot-ball and polo player. Nothing but our anxiety to get home led us to decline his urgent invitation to remain his guest for a fortnight, and enjoy a jungle hunt from the backs of trained elephants. The kindness of the Maharajah did not cease with our visit to the palace, but each day we were the recipients of delicious fruit fresh from his garden, and upon our departure, on May 22, we carried letters of introduction to native gentlemen and officials along our route, who were requested to show us every attention and furnish us desired information which would prove of interest to the readers of the Inter Ocean at home. Still holding to the Grand Trunk road, we set out for Allahabad. The road was lonely and monotonous, and a few miles out from Benares there burst upon us a typical tropical tornado. In a second's time the air was darkened and filled with sand. Striking us from a quarter over our right shoulders, the force of the wind pushed us along at a frightful rate. Sand struck against our goggles with a gritting crunch, filled our nostrils and ears, and forced its way into our mouths. Leaves and twigs struck our faces with stinging force, and shrieking and groaning under pressure of the terrible blasts, the trees along the road threatened every moment to crush us. It was after dusk when the storm subsided, and we found shelter in a village 25 miles away from Benares. On May 27, in Allahabad, we were given an example of India's fiercest heat. Thermometers indoors, under the influence of fans, exhibited 112 degrees, and in the sunlight open the gauge showed 165 degrees, heat almost beyond the comprehension of Americans. We remained but one day in the oven-like hotel, starting at 4 o'clock the next morning, riding until 9, then resting along the roadway until nightfall, making the journey by such easy stages to Cawnpore, "the Manchester of India."

AT MEMORIAL WELL, CAWNPORE.—(See Page 79).

Places of historical interest in Cawnpore are calculated as four in number: first, the site of the government magazine, where Gen. Wheeler, in charge of Cawnpore forces in 1857, should have erected his fortifications of defense; second, the memorial church and the open field south of the structure, where he did assemble his limited force and the refugees; third, the Suttee Chowra ghat, where the massacre of the retiring troops and civilians took place; and fourth and last, Memorial Garden, which commemorates the massacre of the company of women and children, and the well into which the living were cast with the dead. We left Cawnpore on Monday, June 1, for Lucknow, one of the most populous cities of India, situated directly east fifty miles. We sought out the main road without much difficulty, but for the first seven miles we had any amount of trouble, through about as rough and uneven bit of country as one could imagine. As we had left Cawnpore at 5 o'clock in the afternoon, we had run up only 20 miles to our credit ere darkness compelled us to light our lamps. While engaged in this operation our attention was attracted by awful groans at one side of the roadway. Thinking some poor outcast was dying, I selected one of the lamps and proceeded to investigate. A wide ditch barred my progress at the edge of the road, and, mindful of the motto, "Look before you leap," I flashed the cycle lamp rays on the opposite side to select a favorable place to alight. There was none in the immediate vicinity, for as the bright rays penetrated the gloom, they revealed a large, fine cheetah, or panther, crouched in the edge of the brush, his eyes fixed on the glare of my lamp, and his fangs disclosed in excellent array. The sight was a rare one, but as I had learned from books all I cared to know about the habits of wild beasts, I almost broke the lamp in my haste to extinguish it and get the ever-handy 45. Cautiously picking my way back to the wheels, Mrs. McIlrath and I made the chains and sprocket wheels grind out a merry tune to Lucknow.

CHAPTER XVIII.

RACE FOR LIFE WITH A MAD DROVE OF BUFFALO—UNCLE
SAM'S FLAG A FEATURE OF THE QUEEN'S JUBILEE CELE-
BRATION AT DELHI.

It was our idea to see the sights of Lucknow in two days and return to Cawnpore on the evening of the second, but our plans were changed, as Messrs. Thoburn,
Robinson and Mansell, of the American Methodist Mission, called upon us at the
hotel and transferred us, bag and baggage, to the Mission as their guests. Under
their guidance we remained in Lucknow a week. Having returned to Cawnpore,
we resumed our journey on June 11, making rapid progress, principally during
the nights. Ever since entering China, more than a year before, we had seen daily
countless numbers of the hairless, black, water buffalo. Many Europeans fear them
and consider them dangerous, but they treated us with deference until Sunday,
June 20, when we encountered a herd of the fierce-looking, cumbersome beasts
while pedaling our way to Delhi. I do not believe the buffalos had any premedi-
tated intention of attacking us, but as we wheeled slowly through a drove, a calf
became imbued with the idea that bicycles were dangerous. He bolted straight
down the road in front of us, running like a winner for a quarter of a mile. Then
he was attracted by some tempting green leaves, and halted to browse upon them.
As soon as we passed him, the machines which had frightened him became an attraction, and he meekly trotted out and fell in line behind us. The mother, who had
been lumbering along in the rear, became excited at the unusual conduct of her
son, gave a few short snorts, and set out in pursuit. Immediately the entire drove
joined in the novel race, and, with a thundering clatter of hard hoofs ringing in our
ears, we realized that we were being pursued. Faster and faster we spun along,
and as native pilgrims heard the uproar, they gave one glance at the avalanche of
bicycle and buffalo sweeping down upon them and scattered to the right and left.
We tried, by shouting and waving helmets at the calf, to drive him away, but in
vain, and the affair, which had been amusing at first, settled down into a race for
life. It is impossible, as readers know, to take to a tree when on a cycle, so there was
nothing else to do but set a pace for a crazy calf and a drove of jealous buffalo, and
for the next mile and a half we did so. How the calf came to change his mind about
joining his fortune with ours I do not know, but a sudden cessation of the clatter
behind us revealed on sight the calf recumbent in a pool of water, with his sym-
pathizing friends and relatives standing by, grimly looking after us. This was the
outcome of the buffalos' end of the race; ours was garments soaked with perspiration, panting breath, and ourselves so heated and flushed we were dizzy and faint.

The Queen's Jubilee, celebrated the day following our arrival in Delhi, gave us opportunity to enjoy an illumination scene in India, and, though we observed many well-lighted European and government employes' houses, I should not say that the Indian is as much a lover of British rule as the British would have others believe. The usual parade of soldiery and police was the first feature of the evening, and fireworks the final. I thoroughly enjoyed the astonishment caused by the presence of a large American flag, flying from a staff lashed to the life-sized stone elephant which stands in the yard of the government building, and was much amused at the inscriptions on the red cloth banners which the natives hung over their doorways. They read, "Welcome to India;" "Welcome to Delhi," and a rather suggestive few read, "God bless the Prince." It was a few moments before it dawned on me that the inscriptions were originally made to please the eye of the Prince of Wales, when that great functionary of corner-stone laying and baby christening was doing a little globe-trotting at the English public's expense. Who did it, and why that American flag, in all its starry beauty, was flying in front of a government building, were the principal questions asked by army and police officers the next day. Delhi, as a city, was founded during the shadowy ages, which precludes the possibility of dates, but its ruins are visible to-day on an area ten miles wide and fifteen miles long. How often the city has changed its site is only limited to the victories gained by invaders of all tribes and nations. The Rome of Asia, Delhi has known its Nero; Maharrata, Hindoo, Jain, Persian, Afghan, Mohammedan, and the cold, unfeeling Britain, have in turn ruled over the Indian Empire from this ancient city, and the truth has ever been proven that whosoever held Delhi ruled India. Delhi, like many other Indian cities, offers the visitor many interesting buildings of native structure, but so often have we viewed with reverence and awe some superb building, only to learn that it was a tomb for some notable departed, that the word "tomb" has become abhorrent. India will linger in our memory chiefly as one vast group of mausoleums, set in an arid desert and scorched by the fires of a sun fierce as the furnaces of Sheol.

The exposure to heat, from which the Inter Ocean cyclists were suffering daily, led to Mrs. McIlrath's serious condition, which prevented our departure from Delhi on June 24, the day upon which we had made our arrangements to leave. With face swollen so that her eyes were half-closed, her skin was entirely covered with tiny pimples. Small-pox would not have presented a more pitiable sight, but experts pronounced the case prickly heat, and beyond advising perfect rest, cool drinks and hot baths, declared that nothing could be done to drive away or reduce the swelling. Under these conditions we were unable to proceed until July 1, but with the delightful attentions shown us by Mr. and Mrs. Aitkin of the Delhi Morning Post, and Major Mainwaring, of the Native Infantry, time did not hang heavily upon our hands. We swung into the main road at 6 o'clock one morning, taking the Grand Trunk once more, and following its course due north. Karnaul, the city which we should have reached the night before, had it not been for the stiff head winds, we entered at 8 o'clock the following morning, just in time to escape a downfall of rain which detained us until the next day. A second reminder of the plucky little Lenz we found in the register book of the Karnaul dak bungalow, which read, "F. G. Lenze, October 10, 1893, arrived six p. m. Departed six a. m., October 12, American Bicyclist." Strange as it may seem, this was only the second instance in which we found trace of Lenz, though in China, Burmah and India we traveled in all over four thousand miles on identically the same route.

CHAPTER XIX.

PATRIOTISM CURBED JUST IN TIME—BAD NIGHT WITH A FAN-
CIED BITE FROM A COBRA—TWO AMERICAN INVALIDS
TOGETHER IN LAHORE.

From Karnaul we journeyed steadily north, head-winds baffling attempts at speed, and showers and sand storms retarding us for hours. In several instances, we were compelled to journey along the railway line, the rains having swollen the river to such an extent that the roads were flooded. Umballa, a large military station midway between Delhi and Lahore, we reached on the morning of July 3, and again delayed by rain, were forced to spend the glorious Fourth in that city. Unfortunately for me, the dak bungalow was situated within the cantonment lines, and when I arose at daybreak, prepared to fire a salute of twenty-one shots, the gentle-mannered coolie servant gave a terrified look at the gun and bolted for the cook-house. Before I could fire once, a soldier called to me not to shoot unless I wished to be carted off to the guardhouse for violating military orders, which prohibit firing within the cantonment. Undoubtedly I would have been arrested on the charge of discharging firearms inside the lines, creating a disturbance, and possibly treason, and I dread to think of the effect my explanation of celebrating the Fourth of July would have had on an Englishman, especially an army officer, who might have lived on "Cornwallis Road." Rain fell throughout July 5, on which day we were able to cover only eighteen miles, halting for the night at the little vil-lage of Rajpur. Such a small settlement has little need for a dak bungalow, and in consequence, travelers who are so unfortunate as to be compelled to seek shelter for the night, take up quarters at an ancient building owned, but unoccupied, by the Rajah of Petialla. Mrs. McIlrath declared the building was an "old cobra trap," and constantly on the watch for scorpions and snakes, it was but natural that when we retired our dreams were of reptiles.

Several times in the night I was awakened, the last time, along toward morn-ing, by a severe pain in my left leg. Paralyzed with the thought of the deadly krite and cobra bite, and the absolute certainty of death resulting in from five to fifteen minutes, I lay calm and rigid for a moment, thinking I was the victim of a dream, but the smarting in my leg continued, and I called to my wife, exclaiming that I had been bitten. She was awake in an instant, and lighting the lamp, we looked around for the cobra. Though we could find no possible trace of a snake, there were on my leg six small punctures, arranged in a semi-circle. For an hour we waited for indications of snake poison in my system, but none appeared. Several times I imagined the choking sensations which precede complete asphyxia, were attack-ing my throat, but a gulp of water or a puff at my cigarette dispelled this illusion, and at the end of sixty minutes I was compelled to admit that my experience with the cobra had turned out a dismal failure. I cannot to this day offer any possible explanation of my wounds, unless they were inflicted by Rodney, the pet monkey which we made our traveling companion 200 miles back. The "monk" occasionally crept up on my bed to avoid the ants and insects which swarmed over the ground and floors, and it may have been that after making himself comfortable, I had disturbed him and he retaliated by biting the offending leg. Few persons who have not visited India during the Summer rains, can realize what danger there is from poisonous reptiles, chiefly the krite and cobra, and how the dreaded things creep into the most unusual places, just where one would never think of being cautious. In one village of 400 inhabitants, through which we passed, five persons died from snake bites during the five days preceding our arrival. Unlike the rattler, the krite and cobra give no audible warning, except a slight hiss, and directly opposite is the effect of the bite. While the rattler's poison acts on the blood, it may be mitigated by ligation above the wound and the free use of alcohol, but the cobra and krite wounds act directly upon the nerves, producing paralysis and asphyxia, and despite all legends to the contrary, the bite of either reptile, if the fangs are intact, is as surely fatal as decapitation. There is not a remedy known which will even prolong life after the bite has been inflicted.

Cities of considerable size, evidently prosperous and well-kept, are many and frequent along the Trunk road in Punjab, and under an excellent system of irrigating canals, crops appear vigorous and abundant. The native method of raising water from the canals into field-ditches is a novelty to the eyes of the Westerner, and language would never describe the squeaking water wheel, with earthen pots in place of buckets, and the slow-plodding, patient bullocks that revolve the wheel. "Persian Wheels," the primitive machines are called, and though winds are strong and almost perpetual, no one appears to consider the old way inefficient, and harness wind and water with one of the powerful wind engines which dot the prairies of the United States. India is a close second to China in adhering to native customs, and after a journey of fifteen hundred miles, made through the country, in such a manner as to mingle with and know the people, I am of the opinion that the English who govern India, are but a trifle less conservative, and that what broad ideas of improvement they do possess, that would materially improve the natives' condition without benefiting the government revenue, are never allowed to develop and expand. India is not governed by the English with any philanthropic ideas, and when one has spent a few months poring over financial reports and statistics, tax lists and penal codes, the idea is firmly fixed in the mind that India is governed by the English for England.

AT THE DAK BUNGALOW AFTER A LONG RUN. — (See Page 85.)

I have already spoken of the risk a white person incurs in India by being exposed to the rain. Fever is almost certain to follow, and the morning after our arrival in Lahore, I found Mrs. McIlrath with a temperature of 104 degrees, and every symptom of malaria. Though I struggled through the day, caring for her, when I laid down at night, the ache in my muscles and joints, and the fire which raged internally, warned me I was a victim also, and for the next week we lay side by side, comparing temperatures and consoling one another. To be stricken with fever in India is one of the most terrible punishments nature can visit upon the violators of her laws, and all day and all night through we lay without the cooling drinks, the ripe fruits and the delicacies and attentions which ease and encourage the patient at home. By Saturday, July 17, we were able to sit up and totter about the room, and immediately began to obtain strength by carriage rides in the cool evening air.

Lahore does not possess temples, mosques and tombs of great architectural merit, but its chief charm lies in the enormous bazaars which extend for miles through the main streets of the city. The buildings are two-story affairs, built of brick and covered with a staff, which, at a time long ago, was white in color. The shops are merely square rooms, with open fronts; the goods piled on the floors and hung from the ceiling in such a manner as to prevent walking about without danger to stock and inspector. A few of the shops bear sign-boards, painted in English letters. One in particular that attracted my attention, announced that "Subri Lall was a Dentist and Photographer." Another, which struck me as being peculiar, announced that the firm inside sold "fresh salt, patent medicines and millinery."

Some of the characters we met wandering around the bazaars selling charms and fetish bags were most interesting fellows. One gigantic Sikh, who halted at the side of our carriage, displayed his stock in trade to us, and then exhibited his personal gear. Under his tunic he wore a coat and helmet of chain mail; in the belt were seven knives of different sizes, and around the turban were three sharped-edged flat circles of steel, which are thrown in the same manner as a boomerang, and in skillful hands will decapitate an enemy. A stout club, bound with copper, completed the Sikh's outfit, and as I looked upon this mail-clad, walking arsenal, I could but be impressed with how very little was English rule and law respected and feared. Lahore marked the end of our journey along the Grand Trunk road, as from that city on Tuesday, July 20, we turned directly south toward the Persian Gulf and the city of Kurachee. Only thirteen miles of the eight hundred and twenty-four were covered the first evening, and though the two hours of jolting and jarring were keenly felt, when we dismounted at the solitary little station at Kana Kacha, the experience was welcomed. It was home-like, for we had not forgotten our ride across Illinois, Iowa, Colorado, Utah and Nevada on similar paths, usually used by the iron horse and the healthy but indigent hobo. Truly patriotism does assume some homely forms in the American absent from home, but then patriotism is satisfying in any form.

We were now entered on the most dangerous portion of our two thousand miles ride across India. Not only did we abandon all hope for finding an occasional stretch of road, which would afford relief from the monotonous jolt and jar of riding on track ballast, but had made up our minds to expect poor accommodation in the villages along our route. In the face of the heat and obstructions on the road, however, we managed to schedule fifty miles a day before reaching Changa Manga. I met a delightful gentleman in Montgomery, where we spent two days and a night. He was Mr. Fitzherbert, a civil engineer, who had originally landed in India as first officer on a merchantman. I was surprised to learn that a relationship existed between his family and the famous Stonewall Jackson, which fact made us fast friends. Regarding the city in which we were, I can best dismiss the subject in Mr. Fitzherbert's own language:

"Yes," said he, "Montgomery is quite a large place, far different from the little settlement in the desert that I first knew. There are now 4,000 inhabitants, 2,500 are in jail and the balance should be, but as I care little for society that fact does not worry me, and the presence of the city jail assists in making the town. The heat in Montgomery is what renders it almost unbearable. Last year we stood at the head of the list in India, and let me tell you in quiet confidence, that a man that can exist ten years in Montgomery will thoroughly enjoy himself in hell."

Early in the morning of July 28 we said good-bye to our friends in Montgomery, and resumed our grind along the railway line, but we were lonesome no longer. Each train that passed us was manned by a crew who greeted us with cheers and encouraging signals as the train whizzed by, and we humbly and laboriously bucked along over the humps and high spots. From Kacha Khuh we took a run over to Mooltan City, returning to Kacha Khuh by rail. The break in the journey afforded us time to form new and desirable acquaintances, and various little trips, via rail, such as this, furnished us with an insight of a phase of life in India of which we knew nothing before, and which will never cease to be of interest to us—the joys of a traveler on a railway line conducted by the English Government on the English system. In India passengers may be transported in three classes, first, second and third, and as I have yet to learn anything English which is branded first-class and touches the American idea of A 1, we did not for a moment consider the second and third rate inducements of low fare. Purchasing two slips of pasteboard at the "booking office," for which we paid two cents a mile, we were informed that we could take the triangular luggage cases, which we wished to check, into the carriage with us, no goods being checked, but dumped into the "brake van" to be called for and identified by the owner. The first-class carriage was easily identified on the exterior by a coat of white paint, but the first glance into the interior would have led one to believe it was a well-loaded furniture van, on any old day about May 1. Our fellow passengers were a Catholic priest and a lieutenant of Her Majesty's army, and into a space only eight feet long were piled their belongings. I took an inventory and counted five trunks, two valises, four hat-boxes, a wash bowl in a leather case, cane, golf stick, riding whip, four large sun helmets, two rolls of bedding, one bundle of books and a lunch hamper. Arriving at Kacha Khuh, we managed to attract the attention of the guard, who kindly released us, and as we dismounted from the carriage we were convinced that our cycles afforded us just about as great speed, comfort and certainly less inconvenience than the government railway train in India. Truly the Chinese are hide-bound in customs, but the English run them a close race. Though many of their methods are modern, in railways, hotels and conveniences for the public at large, they are far in the rear of the ever-advancing army of modern progress which has its headquarters in the United States of America, and whose generals are the same "wooden nutmeg" inventing Yankees, of whom the English so often speak lightly.

CHAPTER XX.

THE PET MONKEY DINES UPON RUBBER TIRES AND DELAYS
PROGRESS—OFFICIALS REFUSE TO LET THE TOURISTS GO
THROUGH BELOOCHISTAN.

Our last days in India were spent during the monsoon season. The deserts had become lakes of steaming water, the matted undergrowth of rank grass and vegetation rotting, and that we escaped without malarial or typhoid fever was almost a miracle. The railway tracks, which formed our only path, were cut away by the flood of ceaseless rain. The ballast had been swept away and the clay embankment cut into a series of gullies. Four hundred miles we had to push and plod our way through this sticky mass. We left Khanpur on the evening of Aug. 18. The rain had been pouring down for three days, and had subsided into a steady drizzle, which we deemed the most favorable opportunity we would have for a start. We arrived at Daharki, in the plague-stricken district of India, on Aug. 20. We spent the next day, Sunday, at Daharki, and early on the morning of Aug. 22 we started out on a day of mishaps. Before we had passed the yard limits my rear tire collapsed, necessitating a delay of half an hour. Then an unusually long bridge of open structure made our limbs tremble, and scarcely two miles further came a second puncture. Under ordinary circumstances punctures with the outfit and tire we use are trifling affairs, but when each minute counts, as with a race with the sun, such delays are of as great importance to us as any delay to the fire department on its way to a conflagration. Three hours interviewed, when a loud hiss from my rear tire announced a third puncture, and in a few minutes the rim, bumping and smashing on the stone ballast, announced that I was "without air." Three punctures in less than thirty miles was a record to which we were quite unaccustomed. With a third disaster, and no plugs to repair with, my suspicions were aroused and upon investigation I found five large wounds in the tire. As the injury extended along one side only, and that the side which did not come in contact with the ballast, I examined the sides and found the threads torn outward. While sitting on the edge of the railroad ties, gloomily reflecting on the long walk before me, and wondering who could so maliciously have damaged my tire, the pet monkey, Rodney, crawled from his resting place in the bosom of my coat and began plucking grass and herbs. I paid but little attention to him until I heard a sound at the wheel, and turned just in time to discover Rodney chewing a fresh hole. I had caught the offender in the act, and subsequent observations convinced me that he was determined either to make a monkey of us, or satisfy the inexplicable monkey in him. The only reason I failed to kick that grinning ape into space larger than that longed for by the most ardent balloonist, was that he skipped through a barb wire fence quicker than I could reach him with my foot. Mrs. McIlrath carried him into Sarhad, for had he been consigned to my care I fear he would have been cast adrift on the Indus. I reached Sarhad at noon, and had the journey been a mile longer the heat certainly would have killed me. From Sarhad I wired for our trunks and got them after much difficulty. They were billed to a station forty miles ahead, and the station master at first refused flatly to surrender them. He gave them to me after my protests, that without them I should have to walk forty miles more. The plugs were found, the necessary repairs made and at 5 o'clock in the afternoon we were again upon our way.

Lacki Pass, which had been our bugbear for several weeks, proved a serious undertaking, but one which we made with far less inconvenience than we had anticipated. Lacki Pass is the section of railway from Dadu to Lacki. Many persons in discussing our journey had said to us in tones of significance: "Well, just wait until you get to Lacki Pass." Sand of depth and finest quality was the first obstacle we encountered ere we entered the first cutting through stone. The pass would be called a canyon in America, for on one side flowed the broad Indus, then in torrent, and on the other rose the steep, rocky face of the mountain. We decided the momentous question of Lacki Pass by mounting our wheels and cycling along the narrow ledge just outside the rails and next the precipice. Our path was not all that could be desired by novices. It was only a foot in width, beset in places with stones and boulders, with the foaming river hundreds of feet below; but then the Inter Ocean cyclists had long ago passed the novice stage, and we set out at a good pace. Hundreds of water buffalos were scrambling along the rocks at the base of the mountain, or wallowing through the coves of slack water, but excepting the occasions that we dismounted to cross some trestle which spanned a chasm, we had little time to observe scenery. Five miles up the steep grade, a half hour's riding along the dizzy height, and we passed the little station of Bagatara, congratulating ourselves that we were almost into the cuttings which would lead to the plain below. The bend which carried us from the edge of the precipice ended our ride, for we were invited to the home of a Mr. Swetenham, who had come up the tracks behind us on a hand-car. There were three miles more of the pass to cover, but the dinner invitation was too much for us and we loaded our wheels on his hand-car and rolled into Lacki.

ON THE ROAD TO MOOLTAN. — (See Page 88.)

We were a sorry looking pair as we set out on the last short relay in India. The cooking pots which we carried clattered and rattled noisily as they banged against the frames of our bicycles. The luggage cases were heavily laden; our front tires, long ago worn out as rear tires, leaked badly; the cork grips were gone from our handle-bars, and the felt pads of our saddles had become hard as wood. Our attire was thoroughly in keeping with the disreputable appearance of our wheels. Helmets were battered and patched, clothes torn and stained, shoes scuffed and cut to relieve swollen feet, and stockings darned with thread of all colors. Mrs. McIlrath, covered with prickly heat, looked as though bees had stung every portion of her hands and face, and I hardly recognized my own self in the mirror in the gaunt, hollow-cheeked, dull-eyed, yellow-skinned skeleton. Our objective point was Kurrachee. We had a good path, exceptionally free from culverts and bridges, and in the white light of the moon, fanned by the cool breeze from the sea, we sped merrily along until a low-railed bridge obstructed our path, a sign-board indicating that we were but four miles from Dabhugi, the village where we intended to eat our lunch. We were so close upon the bridge before dismounting, that to check my heavy-laden wheel I had to run a few steps with it. Bracing one foot against the curb of the bridge, my eye moved involuntarily to where my foot rested. I was having another encounter with a cobra. The black monster was stretched out in heavy line four feet long. He was of the hooded species, the most deadly of his family, and I stood face to face with death in his most terrible garb. I should have retreated, I should have shot the hideous thing, I should have done anything else but what I did, to stand terrified without power to move a muscle. Suddenly the snake coiled itself into a knot, then twisted around in a circle and disappeared in one of the crevices of the loose rock on the slope of the stream. It was one of the closest escapes I have to relate.

We were in Kurrachee for a week, an attack of fever detaining me. Then began preparation for our trip through Beloochistan, a trip which we did not take. From Kurrachee there is a telegraph line which skirts the coast of Beloochistan and enters Persia. This was the route we had calculated upon since leaving Chicago, and with a view of assisting us to obtain information regarding the conditions of the road, the distances and supply stations, Mr. W. Flowers Hamilton, the United States consular agent, gave a dinner, at which we met a number of British officials and heads of the railway department. These same gentlemen had entertained Lenz on his journey, but when the subject was broached of Mrs. McIlrath and myself making the same trip, great surprise was expressed and the question advanced as to whether or not the government would permit it. "But why should Lenz be permitted to pass through and not ourselves?" I asked of Mr. Barker, the telegraph superintendent. "Things were different then," he replied. "The borders from Cashmere to the gulf are now up in arms, and battles are being fought daily, and not with the most satisfactory result to the government either." This was the first intimation we received that the government would probably interfere with our action. The second came a few days later in a letter from the American Consular Department, which caused me post haste to begin a systematic routine of calls upon the British officials. The letter was dated Sept. 14, and signed by Mr. Hamilton. Briefly, it was a protest against our intention of proceeding to Beloochistan. "I am not a pessimist," he wrote, "and would be the last person to thwart your desires in any way, were there the remotest chance of your safely accomplishing the journey you have planned. I feel, though, that since the natives between this and the Persian frontier are bound to forcibly resist your passage to the territory, that to attempt the journey would mean sudden death to you both, and I earnestly request you to accept my advice and to adopt the alternative route via Bushire, Shiraz, Ispaham, Teheran, Tabriz and Batoum."

I called upon Mr. Wingate, commissioner of Scinde, and Capt. Tighe, and though I used every argument, offering to assume all risks and to relieve the government of any responsibility, their consent of the promise of an indifferent attitude was withheld. "But if I am willing to attempt the journey alone without Mrs. McIlrath?" was my argument. "It is evident that you do not clearly understand the situation," was the reply. "Your life would not be worth one cent ten miles from the border." This was the final argument, and there was nothing for us to do but scratch Beloochistan from the list, and prepare to take one of the British India steamers leaving for Bushire, on Sept. 28.

Our trip through India was severe upon us, physically, and we were compelled to suffer many inconveniences, hardships and even torture from hunger, thirst and weather. There is much misery in India and unalterable condition which forbid that its people ever be benefited by British rule, or that a sympathetic bond be established between the European and Indian. But none who visit its shores will ever have aught to say that both are not hospitable, or that the Englishmen in India do not strive earnestly and sincerely to execute the duties of their office.

CHAPTER XXI.

We took passage on the little coasting steamer "Assyria," leaving Kurrachee on Sept. 28, at 7 o'clock in the morning. There were but two other passengers in the cabin besides Mrs. McIlrath and myself, one a wealthy Arab, the other a missionary of the Reformed Dutch Church. The voyage across the Persian Gulf was colorless and void of incident. Passengers, captain and officers expressed regret that Mrs. McIlrath and I had been so unfortunate in selecting a year which had created so much disturbance in Persia. Scarcity of crops had forced many villagers to subsist by robbery and murder of travelers, and within a single day's journey of the coast hundreds of cases were reported. Politics were affected also, many threats of violence being heard against the Shah and his corps of diplomats. With such a gloomy outlook for a peaceful passage through the wild lands, and the knowledge that winter would overtake us in the mountains of Asiatic Turkey, we had good cause for feeling blue as we sighted the hazy shores which loomed up in the distance on Oct. 8. We anchored three miles off shore, shortly after daybreak. After breakfast, a boat came alongside, the pilot ran up the gang stairs and informed us of the arrival in Bushire of a package of letters. As we were almost destitute, this bit of news made us all the more impatient to be off. Gathering up our boxes, bicycles and the monkey, we shook hands with the genial crew of the "Assyria" and pushed off for Bushire.

To learn that there were no telegrams and news concerning our money, which had been lost in the mails to Kurrachee, would have stunned us had we been anything but American nomads. Bushire did not afford a hotel, and two paupers were forced to look up an Armenian shop-keeper, and persuade him to clear two rooms in an unfinished building, and furnish us with bedding and food during our enforced stay. By sundown on the day of our arrival we were comfortably installed, and though seriously crippled as active participants in the world's tour, we were happy and cheerful. Though the community of foreigners in Bushire was small, there is a certain sympathetic bond between all which renders the circle delightful, and as all welcome a new arrival with outstretched arms, we found our stay in the town a very pleasant one. We were dined by Mr. Ferguson and Mr. Churchill, of the Interior Bank of Persia; Surgeon Captain Lumsden, Mr. J. Meyer and Col. Mead, the British Consul General. We also enjoyed a delightful little "tiffin" with Mr. Christmas, of the Indo-European Telegraph Company's inspection corps, and all of these gentlemen united in preparing us for our journey inland. As the first and second steamers arriving from India brought no news of our lost money, we finally gave up all idea of restoration, and deciding that a longer wait was impracticable, made preparation to start at once, having communicated by cable with our American resources. After a week of laying in stores, supplies and heavy clothing, obtaining passports, permits to sleep in telegraph stations, and letters of introduction, we bade adieu to our friends on Nov. 8, and following in the rear of a gang of coolies, started forth to Teheran.

ON DECK OF THE STEAMSHIP "ASSYRIA." — (See Page 94).

The journey from Bushire to Teheran may be divided into three complete stages: first, from Bushire to Shiraz, 173 miles; thence to Ispahan, 312 miles; then on to Teheran, 285 miles. To cycle from Bushire to Shiraz is quite as impossible as to cycle up the side of Pike's Peak. The elevation often reaches 6,000 feet and the road is a mass of boulders and deep sand. The ascent is not gradual, but a continuation of terraces called "kotals" by the Persians, and in these kotals donkeys are the only creatures which can safely walk and carry burdens. Our path lay through uninhabited sand desert, with not a tree or shrub visible. Walking over unbroken road by the side of a patient and heavily-laden mule is as tiresome as it is monotonous, and we were a badly used pair when we arrived at Kushub, the end of our first day's journey in Persia. Resuming the trip the next morning, we soon caught up with a caravan of three score mules, laden with shiny tin cases of petroleum, which bore the welcome brand, "made in the United States." Our forces now consisted of more than fifty men, the majority armed with muzzle-loading rifles, a few with pistols and the remainder with clubs having iron knobs at the end. We felt then sufficiently strong to resist the robbers, against whom we had been warned. The bandits first manifested themselves when the caravan was stopped, and the head muleteer asked for a "present." I was astounded to find that the robbers were none other than a few soldiers who were supposed to be guarding a little village we had passed some miles back. As the "present" is always cash, and often demanded at the muzzle of a gun, the courts of any civilized country would probably call such proceeding highway robbery, but in Persia, where troops are unpaid at under-paid rates, and often go ragged and hungry for years, the laws cannot be supposed to be of superior standing to the army. Toward Mrs. McIlrath and me the unkempt rascals were civil enough, but persisted in detaining the muleteers. I suppose the basis of a "present" was finally agreed upon, for the orders were given to push on after a brief delay. We were slightly in advance of the caravan, continuing our way among the boulder-strewn foothills, when just about daybreak, three men sprang from behind rocks and halted us. They demanded money. Our servant was slightly in advance of Mrs. McIlrath and me, and he promptly pushed a 45-calibre revolver under the nose of the leader. The second man looked into my rifle, and in less than ten seconds so many gun locks clicked behind my back that I feared one would be discharged by accident, and the boy and myself perforated as well as the bandits. It was evident from the manner of the trio that they realized that they had made a mistake, but whether the mistake lay in the fact that we were well armed, or that we were foreigners, was not made clear. They declared themselves soldiers, who only wished a "present" and when I refused to accept their explanation, they protested that they were honest men, but hungry. Such might have been the case, but we gave them nothing except advice that they sell their guns and buy bread. An attempt on the part of a second trio of men, encountered a few days later, to obtain a contribution, resulted in an exhibition of spunk by Mrs. McIlrath. The leader had seized the bridle of her mule, and startled her to such an extent that she poked the muzzle of her revolver into the fellow's face. The villain released his grip and apologized profusely for not having recognized us as Europeans. They seemed to think that so long as they robbed only the natives, they committed no crime.

We halted at Diriz on Oct. 12, having been on the road for twelve hours without food. The muleteers, for some reason, probably anxiety to fulfill their contract and be through with us, protested against the delay, urging that we could find neither food, water nor shelter in the place. I had learned by this time that the low caste Persians are born liars, and insisting upon the stop, we found, just as we had expected, both food and water. We refreshed ourselves, and two hours later proceeded at snail-like pace across the plain to Kazeroon. We spent three days in this city, the guests of Mr. Marker, an excellent type of the educated Armenian, who furnished us with much information and took care to see that we were started on our journey in proper form. Wearied by the fatigue of sleepless days and monotonous journeying by night, we changed our hours for travel when we left Kazeroon, taking our departure at 8 o'clock in the morning. One of the most laborious tasks of our entire journey was now before us. Climbing the Alps is nothing compared with the ascent of the kotals in Persia. The muleteers know nothing of scenery, and do not even know the names of villages only a half a mile from the beaten path. But they do know that delays cause great annoyance, and they keep you constantly at the best speed you are capable of making, lest some descending caravan meet you and confusion ensue. One of the mules, upon which was loaded Mrs. McIlrath's bicycle, backed into a huge boulder which jutted into the road, breaking the fork and rendering it unfit for use. Friday, Nov. 19, the road into Shiraz, began to take on a fairly smooth appearance, whereat I lost no time in oiling up my bike. As I prepared for a stiff run into Shiraz, Mrs. McIlrath, contemplated her damaged machine, and expressed a wish that the mule had died the day before she entrusted her wheel to his care. Two miles of fairly level road enabled me to distance the horde of rough riders. Caravan after caravan my cycle passed, not pausing until I whizzed down the main street of Shiraz, arriving three hours ahead of my party.

A native mechanic repaired Mrs. McIlrath's wheel, though it took him eight days to do so, giving us ample time to make friends in the city. One would be difficult to please who could not enjoy life in Shiraz. Dr. Sculley and Mr. Wood, superintendent of telegraphs, alternated in dinners; Mr. Von Rijkon, an adopted American, entertained us at lunch, and in each European home we sipped afternoon tea, were entertained with music and listened to delightful little stories of Persian life. With friends we made several excursions about the city, bartering in the bazaars, visiting the places of interest and calling upon Persians of high rank. Our sight-seeing in Shiraz was ended on Wednesday, Dec. 1, when we departed for the north. Our cyclometer revealed that we covered twenty-three miles by dusk over sandy roads and in the face of strong winds, the first day out from Shiraz. At Zerghun we halted for the night, and were up and away before daybreak the next morning. By 10 o'clock we could see outlined against the blue mountains to the north, a village which we knew to be Kinorah, a small, harmless little settlement, where we had been advised to seek accommodations. The ruins of Persopolis are near by, and wishing to visit the grandest monument of a kingly ruler's power that the modern world knows, we wheeled into Kinorah, where we were the guests of the Rev. W. A. Rice.

CHAPTER XXII.

AT THE RUINS OF PERSEPOLIS—AN AUTOGRAPH ON THE PORCH OF XERXES—LOST IN A SNOWSTORM AND MRS. McILRATH'S FEET FROZEN.

Describing the ruins of an ancient city, a famous structure, or even a locality, which, to the modern world, is vaguely grasped as having an existence, is a task most difficult. Consequently I shall in no manner attempt to enter detail in describing the ruins of Persepolis. Towering forty-five feet above the plain the grand platform extends 1,500 feet north by south, and, far as the excavations of explorers have revealed, 800 feet east and west. The first of the remarkable remnants of Achæmenian glory which greet one, are the pieces which form the group known as the Porch of Xerxes. The portals are the favorite background upon which visitors inscribe their names. I have always held such proceeding as vandalism, and thought the names of British ambassadors, naval officers, and clergy deface the rock. I should have foregone the pleasure of perpetuating our visit, had not my eye fallen upon the following inscription: "Stanley, New York Herald, 1870." Never for a moment has an inhabitant of Chicago allowed that New York to thrust its ancient claim upon the world as a typical American city without resentment, and immediately we chipped beneath, "McIlrath, Chicago Inter Ocean, 1897."

Our tour of the ruins was thorough, including visits to the grand hall of Xerxes, the hall of One Hundred Columns, and the tombs of Darius and Xerxes, south of the Grand Platform. Persepolis, as it stands to-day, is a stern rebuke to him who styled himself "King of Kings" and "Ruler of the Rulers of the Universe," and vowed that he would build a city that would be the capital of the world, and peopled by all tribes until time nevermore. On Sunday, Dec. 4, we resumed our journey up the hills toward Dehbid. The roads were muddy and the various streams swollen, and we encountered rainstorms and high winds, which caused us to lose the path and occasioned us much discomfort before we could enter the town of Murghab. We found the hotel crowded with passengers, many of whom had seen us previously. There was one Persian in the number who evidently wished to speak to me concerning Frank Lenz, since he uttered the boy's name, pointed to the bicycle, and drew his finger across his own throat in a manner suggestive of Lenz's horrible fate. Monday, Dec. 6, our journey, though not extensive, was exhaustive; we walked up grades too steep to permit of riding, and we walked down grades too steep and rough to ride with safety. Occasionally we passed through sections of country where patches of snow glistened under the shade of bushes and wild grass. From Khan-I-Khergan our ride was a steady up-hill grind for several miles, but ended when the summit was gained by a four-mile dash downgrade into the little settlement of Dehbid. When we left the following morning we had the wind at our back and made such excellent time that we entered the dreaded Koli-kush before we realized it. We experienced no difficulty in the pass, riding down the opposite side as easily as we had ascended the southern approach. There is little to tell of our ride into Surmek, except that we made it at the rate of fifteen miles an hour. The scenery in the background was rugged and outlined against the clear blue sky was beautiful. The high fever which Mrs. McIlrath developed in consequence of a drenching, caused the loss of a day in Abadeh, but it gave me an opportunity of visiting the bazaars and inspecting the marvelous work done by the wood-carvers. We cycled from the telegraph station on Dec. 11, bound for Maksudbeg, seventy-one miles north. We found the roads in passable condition and were escorted for eight or ten miles by a Mr. Stevens, who is connected with the telegraph company, and the solitary cyclist of Central Persia. Passing through the cities of Shulgistan and Yezbikhast, we should have made Maksudbeg early in the afternoon, but I discovered three large lacerations in my rear tire, which prevented fast riding.

The "Khaneh" at Maksudbeg was well filled the night of our arrival, but until our baggage train and interpreter arrived we lacked for nothing. We left Maksudbeg early the next morning, whirling at a rapid rate to Marg, where we stopped for the night. On Tuesday, Dec. 14, when we again set out for Julfa, we completed within thirteen miles the second of the three long stages into Teheran. Though many Persians reside in Julfa, the town is typically Armenian. The same high walls that are so general in Persian cities, face each street, but the buildings inside are Armenian, the inscriptions over the doors are in Armenian characters, and the majority of the people seen on the street are Armenians. The Armenian men are a type in themselves. They appear dirtier than the Persian, and if circumstances permit, they affect European clothes and get beastly drunk. In occupation, the Armenian finds himself adapted to any business or trade and in general transactions is a fluent liar and barefaced cheat. There are few good Armenians, but there are those who have received a liberal education, or have been taken in hand by kindly people and brought up to Christian and civilized ideas. The other good Armenians are like the good American Indians—they are deceased Armenians. At Ispahan we were the guests of Bishop Stuart, of the Church of England Mission. Ispahan is just across the Landah River from Julfa, and is not so void of features. Having visited, at his palace, His Royal Highness, the Zil-i Sultan of Persia, the Armenian Cathedral, and the brass working bazaar of Ispahan, we departed for the North on Saturday, Dec. 19. We had a long, hard ride over ravines strewn with rocks, to the city of Soh, where we were the guests of Mr. Newey, an intimate friend of Mr. Christmas, whom we met in Bushire. Snow began to fall on Dec. 22, and our entertainer refused positively to allow us to proceed. The storm did not cease until the following morning, when, despite the protests of Mr. Newey, we set out for the village of Khurud, twenty-five miles away, and a most disastrous trip it proved to be. We expected to cover the distance to Khurud by 4 o'clock in the afternoon, but when that hour arrived our cyclometers registered but eight miles, and we were worn out and almost unable to proceed farther. We had prepared for the trip by putting on extra sweaters and incasing our legs in heavy woolen leggings, such as are worn by native travelers, but we found, after a mile or so on the road, that the most discomfort we suffered was with our hands and feet. Beneath the snow were many pools of water, and into these we floundered, wetting ourselves to the knees and our bicycles to the hubs.

A ROCKY PASS THAT BARRED OUR WAY.—(See Page 98.)

As a wild, precipitous descent lay between us and the village, and as nightfall was fast approaching, Mrs. McIlrath suggested that I leave her and the machine in the first gorge which afforded any shelter, and then hurry forward, find the village and send back men and horses for herself and the wheels. I did not entertain the thought for a moment, for I was too deeply impressed with the trying situation, though I did not let her know of our danger. For a time I succeeded in buoying up her spirits, but as we slowly plodded through canyon after canyon, the winds ever growing colder and the sun sinking from sight, Mrs. McIlrath refused to be comforted and grew weaker and more erratic in her movements. The effect of the high, rare air, the terrible mental strain and the enormous muscular exertion were the greatest test to which I have ever been put. It was necessary that we keep moving, and with such an object in view I whistled and sang, and finally scolded Mrs. McIlrath in language most harsh. It would have been cowardly to have been unkind toward my wife under such circumstances had not the occasion demanded, and the cross words intended to assist in working out our salvation. There was no time or thought to be wasted, and I used every means to urge her onward. Cruel as it may seem to those who do not know the dire result of falling exhausted in the snow, I looked about for something with which to flog my wife did she refuse to proceed, and had decided to use the heavy leather belt which encircled my waist. I shouted to her constantly to keep her toes moving, and to bend her feet as much as possible. For two hours we floundered on, and I was then forced to pile the machines together in a conspicuous place, which could afterward be found, and leaving them, push on unhampered. Up the canyon we plunged, every step an agony and every hundred yards a mile to our tortured minds. I kept my wife in front, dreading lest she should fall and succumb to the dreadful fatigue which ends in death.

So absorbed was I in her safety, that I lost track of the telegraph poles, and was suddenly confronted with the realization that we were lost on the very peak of the mountain. My medicine case contained no liquors or stimulants, and we had not tasted food since 7 o'clock in the morning. There were but two chances for our lives. Our interpreter had gone on ahead with his horse and our luggage. He might send out a rescue party for us. The second chance was a more forlorn one. At 9 o'clock each evening the telegraph line between Bushire and Teheran is tested, and if communication is broken, the officer on each side of the break will send out men for an immediate repair. It lacked a full half hour to the testing time, and I determined to wait fifteen minutes and then if help did not arrive, climb the pole, shoot the insulators from the arms, and break each and every wire. The fifteen minutes passed and I was in search of the telegraph pole, with but ten minutes to interrupt the "test." In the gloom I perceived a number of dark figures, which I took to be wolves. As they came nearer they developed into men and horses, and from the cheery manner in which the riders greeted us we knew that the interpreter had not forgotten us, and had sent to our rescue.

It would have been Mrs. McIlrath's duty as a woman to have fainted when the horses arrived, but she did nothing of the kind. She thanked God, as I did, and when placed in the saddle, wrapped herself in blankets and ordered the men to "hurry up" just as if we had been waiting for them by appointment. Slowly we descended the tortuous path, the intelligent horses leading the men until the right road was regained. I called to my wife to ascertain her condition, and she assured me that her feet no longer pained, but were "warm and comfortable." Two hours later, when we halted at the Chapar Khaneh, my wife cried to me piteously that she could not walk, and I knew only too well why her feet had been "warm and comfortable." We carried her into the dim-lighted post-room and cut the leggings from her limbs. The shoes were ice-covered and stiff. The blackness of her stockings ended at the ankles, and the foot casings were white frost. My instructions to the men were to rub her feet with snow, until each toe showed its natural ruddy glow to a candle light held behind it. For two hours they kept up a vigorous massage, and then when the power of motion was restored and swelling was noticeable, I was content to leave the rest to nature. Two men on horses went up the slopes of the mountain next day and brought in the cycles. The cyclometer was frozen so tightly that at the first revolution of the wheel it had broken off. Otherwise the machines were unharmed. It was absolutely necessary that we reach a point which would afford communication with the nearest surgeon, and on Friday we wrapped Mrs. McIlrath in blankets and placed her upon a horse, our destination being Kashan, a telegraph station. We were in the saddle ten hours before we sighted the city. The telegraph operator was an Armenian, drunk as he could be, and after questioning me as to my ability to speak and understand English, he permitted us to occupy the waiting room.

I sent in haste a message to Dr. Wishard, superintendent of the American Presbyterian Mission at Teheran, informing him that my wife's feet were frozen. He replied that he would do all he could, coming himself or sending medicines as we pleased.

CHAPTER XXIII.

We lingered three days at Kashan before the preliminary treatment of my
wife's feet permitted us to proceed. Here we spent our Christmas Day, dejected
and home-sick. In vain we searched the bazaars for a turkey, goose, or duck for our
Christmas dinner, but as if to recompense us for our earnest efforts to celebrate, a
ragged coolie brought us a rabbit, and with turnips in lieu of sweet potatoes, we
endeavored to deceive ourselves into believing we had enjoyed a good old-fashioned Southern feast. We left Kashan in the native "khagvar," two shallow boxes
placed on a mule's back, the boxes laden equally to balance the load on either side.
We placed Mrs. McIlrath on one side, her bicycle, luggage case and bedding in
the opposite box, and on Tuesday, Dec. 28, resumed our journey. The first night
of our stop on the way to Koom the owner of the khadgavar refused to continue
on the journey without an increase to the contract price for the rent of his mule.
Mrs. McIlrath's condition would not admit of a delay, and I was compelled to
resort to the extreme measures used in China in such a case, and with success, for
within ten minutes we were again on the road. While stopping at a tea house for
refreshments on Dec. 29, our little caravan was overtaken by three of the Sultan's
cavalrymen. They were inclined to twit us on the effort required to propel bicycles,
and I challenged them for a race. Although Mrs. McIlrath required my attention
hourly, she entertains such contempt for those who despise cycling, that it was at
her request that I left her behind to engage in the test of speed with the horse-sol-
diers. I left the three troopers easily in the rear after their steeds had begun to
show signs of fatigue, never for an instant slackening my pace until I flashed into a
village eight miles from the starting point. I had regained my composure, smoked
several cigarettes and idled away half an hour ere the horsemen appeared on the
brow of a hill one mile away. Though the riders were breathless, their horses reek-
ing with foam, when they halted in front of the tea house, not a look or a word
betrayed their chagrin, and they proffered tea and cigarettes with good grace but
with great dignity. Not satisfied with the one defeat, the captain demanded that I
overtake him ere the next stage. They had a good half hour's start of me, because
I waited for Mrs. McIlrath's arrival. As soon as she assured me of her comfortable
condition, I sprang into saddle, and settled down into a gait which carried me nine
miles into an open valley, just in time to sight the three horsemen and the city of
Pasangoon in the distance. The horsemen must have sighted me as soon as I did
them, for when I next looked up the trio had separated and were strung along the

road in Indian file. I strained every muscle to the utmost, but the up-grade, the load of camera, revolvers, luggage case and monkey had been too great, and I only succeeded in overtaking one of the trio. The other two had not dismounted when I reached the Chapar Khaneh, and were loud in their greeting and praise of the "asp-i-chubee," as they called the bicycle.

MR. McILRATH AND PARTY AT DASHEN TAPPI.—(See Page 105.)

We were up before daybreak Dec. 30, dismayed to find the ground covered with snow, and pushed into Koom by nightfall, just in time to escape the most violent end of a storm, which delayed us for two days. Proceeding by caravan was out of the question, and as Koom afforded nothing in the medicine line, we were obliged to make the remaining stage by "diligence" to Teheran. Though the trip can be accomplished with ease in less than twenty-four hours, the exorbitant sum of $26 was demanded for fare. The conveyance which bears such a high-sounding name is simply a prairie schooner, hauled by four horses ranged abreast. It is a "terror" as a conveyance, the jolts and jars sending one high into the air, making conversation impossible, while the rattle of the crazy vehicle is like that of volleys of musketry. When we had accomplished about six miles the driver deliberately guided the horses into a deep snow-drift, informed us that progress was impossible, and threats, argument and persuasion would not induce him to proceed. Finding he would not yield, we became equally stubborn, and would not allow him to return, as he proposed, until the next day, when he predicted the passage would be more probable. Unfortunately Mrs. McIlrath and I were weary, and while we slept the cowardly driver cut the horses and quietly decamped. How long we should have remained in this predicament is difficult to conjecture, had not a carriage arrived from the north, containing as passengers Mr. J. P. Whiton Stuart, of New York, and his secretary. Mr. Stuart at once volunteered to send for the horses which had abandoned our vehicle, effect a change of driver and animals and thus help us on our way. This was done, but not until the afternoon had so far advanced that only one stage was accomplished in the entire day.

We passed a miserable night Jan. 2, 1898, in the stables of the Post House in Hassinabad. Getting an early start we arrived at Kah-rizak, twenty-six miles north, in the afternoon. It was then but a short ride to the mosque and shrine called "Shah Abdullah Azim," where we boarded a steam railway for Teheran, eight miles ahead. We were then in the capital of Persia, snow-bound and unable to proceed, even had weather permitted, on account of Mrs. McIlrath's feet, but thankful, for Teheran afforded hospitals and surgeons, and best of all, American ones.

The city of Teheran has been the imperial residence since Shah Aga Mohammed Kahn, founder of the Khajar dynasty, which now reigns, chose to elevate the insignificant village to a place of royal abode, and bestowed upon it the titles, "City of the Shadow of God," and "Footstool of the King of Kings." We visited the magnificent palace of the reigning Shah, Muzaffaru-ud-din, and also made a tour to Dashen Tappi, one of his favorite resorts. In this latter tour our party consisted of Mr. Black, Mr. Morris and myself, three cyclists; two horsemen, Messrs. Warner and DeMunk; and Misses DeMunk and Warner, and Mrs. McIlrath, entrusted to the care of a Cossack, who drove a pair of mules attached to a heavy Russian carriage. Owing to the condition of Mrs. McIlrath's extremities we were unable to accept many invitations, but despite the fact, we left Teheran greatly indebted to the members of the European Colony there. When we departed on Feb. 25, it was by the carriage, as cycling to Resht was entirely out of the question, the roads being deep with snow and the passes in the mountains ice-bound. There is little to write of the journey in Persia. Scenery was either a vast plain, studded with sage-brush, or the panorama was that of a barren, dull rock which had neither rugged beauty nor picturesque formation. Three days of this monotonous travel brought us to Kasbin, where we were delayed by more wretched weather until March 6. More snow fell directly we took to the road, our path often taking us along the edge of a precipice the entire slope of which, above and below us, was glaring ice. A slip or a false step meant certain death, and each instant that an iron-shod hoof grated and crushed, we expected to hear a wild shriek and the crash of a fatal fall. At one point on the journey we passed a party of laborers at work rescuing from the bottom of the gorge a horse and rider, both stiff in death. This was but one of the many horrors on the road to Resht, which we reached on March 13. The city affords two hotels, both conducted by Frenchmen, and as we inquired for the best, we were directed to one designated as the Hotel Europe. I would recommend any reader contemplating a trip to Resht to apply for lodgings at the other hotel. Our knowledge of the French language was limited, but though we had absorbed sufficient to enable us to eat heartily and sleep soundly in French, we felt certain of success at the Europe Hotel. The avaricious design of the frowsy proprietor foiled us, however, and as his rates were $8 a day, we made our stay in the city as short as possible.

CHAPTER XXIV.

CYCLISTS LAND IN RUSSIA—TIFLIS, "THE PARIS OF THE CAU-
CASUS"—IN SIGHT OF MOUNT ARARAT—SUICIDE OF THE
PET MONKEY.

We left Resht Monday, March 21, on board the nondescript steamer "B." There were but two cabins afforded by the steamer, and to one of these Capt. Ahrninckie assigned the Inter Ocean tourists. The run to Baku is less than the Chicago-Milwaukee or Cleveland-Detroit runs, but owing to delays we did not reach Baku until Thursday, March 24. We formed a number of friends in the city, dinners, teas and drives being of daily occurrence. We also attended the opera, but as great as was our diversion, we pined for the days that we should again be in the saddle, with our feet upon the pedal. Our Easter Sunday of 1898 we spent in Tiflis, the quaintest of all Russian cities. Tiflis is called the "Paris of the Caucasus," but the real significance of the name is "Hot Springs." Hot Springs there are at Tiflis, not of valuable mineral nature, but most grateful to the weary traveler who visits the bath-houses, and after a thorough steaming is kneaded into supple activity by Persian attendants. Here, of all the cities on earth, I do not know of any one which will afford the visitor more varied and interesting street scenes. New Orleans, when in the regalia of its annual Mardi-Gras, is not more picturesque. It is not only the fanciful appearance of the street, but the unique procession of pedestrians, men of all nations, that makes Tiflis and its streets appear like the dancing room of a bal masque. The Russian and the natives of the Caucasus are more hospitable than any people we ever met. Officials of the city heaped upon us courtesies and seemed to enter into a contest with each other in paying us attention. The last few days of our stay in Tiflis were unusually busy. The ruined tires of Mrs. McIlrath's bicycle and the badly damaged front tire of my own had to be replaced by new ones, and the best we could make out was to purchase inner tubes and alter our old tires to suit the available article. We left Tiflis on April 14, many friends being present to see us off. We were all happy, even including Rodney, the monkey, to be again awheel. I should mention that it was not until after our sojourn in Tiflis that Mrs. McIlrath was able, for the first time since her horrible night in the mountains of Persia, to put her feet again to the pedals of her machine. Lost twice on the road, and with many an inconvenience and delay, an account of which would be but to go over in part our misfortunes in other climes, we arrived during the latter part of April at Ahkty, 60 miles from Mount Ararat, the most famed mountain in the world's history, the resting place of the ark in which Noah preserved the family, human animal, reptile and winged.

The day after our arrival in Ahkty was a fete day in Russia, the birthday of the Grand Duke. The town was rich in color with the red, blue and white flags, the shops were closed and bands played in the park. Troops in dress uniform swarmed the streets; women and children in holiday clothes promenaded through the groves of trees 'neath the window of our hotel; and above all, shown in glittering, lofty beauty Mount Ararat, immaculate and cold as if, since her duty done in receiving the ship of God, she had locked herself in frigid mail against the frivolous people beneath.

An oil-laden tramp steamer, after three days of wallowing along the shores of Asia Minor, placed us in Constantinople on June 9. We had been directed to several hotels in the city, but as our informants had confessed that all were uniformly piratical in their practices, we selected one directly opposite the American Consulate. Galatea, the section of the city in which we landed, is the water front and wholesale commercial portion of the town, and as we threaded our way through the crowded street, following closely the coolies who carried our luggage, we had excellent opportunity of witnessing the sights of the most interesting quarter of the great city. To those who have not visited the interiors of China, India, Burmah and Persia, Constantinople may appear truly Oriental, but to the Inter Ocean cyclists the city presented anything but a resemblance to manners and customs Eastern. We spent seven days in diligent search for curious sights, and of them all we decided that the most attractive features were the Salaamlik, or public reception at prayer by the Sultan; "the dogs of Stamboul" and Constantinople, the fires and fire department, and the museum and the tomb of Alexander. The religious day of Mussulmans is Friday, and we were present when Abdul Hamid, the Sultan, wended his way to the mosque to pray. The populists turned out to greet him, and soldiers flashed their way through the streets; it was a gala day in Constantinople. We saw the face of the Sultan squarely, but it did not please us. If it were possible for human face to resemble a hawk, the Sultan of Turkey certainly bore that resemblance to the cruel bird. The eyes were glittering, the brows big and slanting, the nose hooked, and the lips thin and compressed. The face was not one to be forgotten. Features do not always bespeak the character of a man, but, after looking into the eyes of the Sultan, one could readily understand how such a man could order the extermination of the opposing sect of a religious people, and calmly read the report of his subordinates who informed him that 3,500 of his Armenian subjects had been slain in the streets of Constantinople and Stamboul in less than thirty-six hours.

Fires are a serious event in Constantinople, much more so than my American brethren, in whose country conflagrations are daily affairs, can well imagine. The city, with its sea breeze, the hills and valleys as a flue, and with houses of wood, and streets so narrow that flames overreach, a fire, with ordinary start, has an advantage which only exhaustion and skill will overcome. As we saw for ourselves, "exhaustion" is the only method of the Constantinople firemen. There is so much ceremony about going to a fire that the chief and his men are well nigh put out by fatigue before the blaze is extinguished. When I say extinguished, I mean before the fire burns itself out. It is prevented only from being a conflagration by the fact that those members of the department not laid out for want of breath, and assisted by zealous citizens, grab long poles and push and pull down the adjacent buildings. "The dogs of Stamboul" are numbered by the thousands. They are quiet and well behaved, do not bark at wagons and pedestrians, and sleep on the sidewalk, in the gutter and in the middle of the street. They are the scavengers of the city, and woe to the man who abuses them. Sleeping by day, they wake into activity as night advances and the shops close. Meat markets, restaurants, bakeries, private residences and hotels throw the leavings from counter and table into the gutters, and the dogs "do the rest."

I must record, while in Constantinople, the untimely death of Rodney, the monkey. The following quotation appeared in the Servet of Constantinople, and is a fair example, at the same time, of a Turkish newspaper joke: "Suicide at the Maison Tokatlian.—Effendi McIlrath, an American journalist, who is resting at the Maison Tokatlian, is completing a remarkable journey through the interior of Asia and Europe, using bicycles to transport himself and wife. The sights of Constantinople have proven so attractive that the gentleman has had little time to devote to a pet monkey, which has been his companion for several thousand miles. After sunset of the past day the monkey was left alone in the gentleman's room, and upon returning from dinner the master found the animal hanging by his neck from the window sash. As no papers were left and no warning given, jealousy is ascribed as the cause, but the police will investigate."

I do not know that jealousy was the cause of the little fellow's self-inflicted end, but I am inclined to believe that the desire to reach some strawberries which lay upon the table near him, the twisting of the strap on his neck, and the consequent choking, had more to do with the ending of Rodney's erratic career.

We departed for Constantza, Roumania, Saturday, June 18, on one of the coasting steamers carrying mail and passengers to the Oriental express, bound for Paris via Buda-Pesth and Vienna. I would not attempt to fix the date when Roumania was populated, but during the ages when Romans required visitors to do as Romans did, the toga-clad nation utilized Roumania as a sort of ancient Australia, a dumping-ground for incorrigible criminals. Some of the hotel and restaurant keepers in Roumania at the present day should be able to trace their ancestry without trouble. The traits of the pioneers are still exhibited. Constantza is pretty; it is one of those white, clean little places which only exist on the sea fronts where coal dust, soot and factories and black dust is unknown. It is called the "Brighton of Roumania," but since the water off Long Island is just as salt, and the hotel prices almost as exorbitant, the name might be improved on.

We selected the Hotel Union in Bucharest as our stopping place, but scarcely had we entered the corridors one evening than a crowd hemmed us in and began the usual catechism in the three popular languages, French, German and Roumanian. Though I managed to slip Mrs. McIlrath through the crowd and up to her chamber, I was unable to leave the throng until two hours later. The next day we were visited by the various members of the "Clubul Ciclistilar Bucharest," which means Bucharest's Cycling Club, and, after luncheon with some of the English-speaking members, we were made honorary members of the organization. Principally Germans, the club is a jolly set. They were our guides, companions and entertainers during our sojourn in the city. They sent flowers to Mrs. McIl-rath, dined us, invited us to their meetings, and presented us with souvenirs of the occasion. We fared well in the city, and our ride over the miserable roads was the chief topic in cycling circles. It is inconceivable to me why a country so intensely interesting as Roumania, a city so wickedly fascinating and beautiful as Bucharest, should be so little frequented by travelers. Paris, with all its world-wide reputation as a city of gold-plated vice, cannot compare with the more obscure Bucharest. Lovers of beautiful architecture will find in the palaces, museum and academy all that they desire; admirers of glittering uniforms and lovely women will be able to feast their eyes each evening, when all the capital turns out in dress parade on the beautiful boulevarde; artists will find quaint characters, costumes, landscapes and romantic homes, and the novelist of Zolaism will be able to weave plots of realism that will horrify the morals and titillate the perverted palate of the sen-sation-loving gourmand. As a kingdom, Roumania enjoys liberties which are not to be equaled in any republic extant. The press is free to the extent that monarch and private character, private history and personal characteristics are not exempt from type. Were American editors to write as do their Roumanian brothers, the vocation would be one excluded from the lists of acceptable risks of life insurance companies. Rains delayed our departure from Bucharest until Sunday, July 26. We were escorted on our start from the city, at 1 o'clock in the afternoon, by Messrs. Furth and Jensen, two of the most hardy road riders of the Bucharest Cycling Club, and we whirled off thirty-one kilometers ere we entered Ploesti, the half-way stop.

CHAPTER XXV.

A curious and confusing method of road measurement exists in Roumania, by which many cyclists are led to believe distances are far less than is really the case. If the official distance from village A to E is given as 100 kilometers, that sum does not include the distance inside the boundaries of villages B, C and D. Thus a day's run through a dozen straggling settlements involves riding a total of 80 kilometers more than maps and road posts indicate. We found this difficulty to exist on our first day's run from Bucharest. When we reached Siniai the total mileage indicated was 82, yet we had six kilometers to travel ere we halted at the hotel in the center of the town. Siniai is not a city of trade and industry. It is a mountain summer resort, made popular twelve years ago by an eccentric Roumanian prince, and perpetuated by Carol I., King of Roumania, who selected the enchanting hills as the royal summer palace. The palace is called Pelesu Castle, and, as the English-speaking proprietor of our hotel told us that visitors were freely admitted, we pressed him into service as guide, and made a visit to the abode of royalty. We discovered His Majesty on a terrace in front of the castle, playing with two chubby children. I was fearful lest he see us and regard our presence as an intrusion, but assured by our guide that the monarch was not in the least sensitive about strangers, we passed toward the distinguished group. As we neared the king he stood erect, and looked at us intently, and as he raised one finger to salute by touching the side of his military cap, he spoke clearly, "Guten morgen." The little prince straightened up, brought his boot heels together so that the bare calves of his fat legs touched, and, imitating the sovereign, he piped, "Guten morgen." The king had mistaken us for Germans, his own nationality.

When we departed from Siniai we left behind us one of the most romantic and beautiful of cities. Our route was slightly up-hill for the first twenty-five kilometers, but with excellent roads, cool air and frequent shade we did not feel any discomfort and rode rapidly. It is tantalizing to other cyclists and tourists for one to write of elegant roadways, delightful scenery and charming little roadside inns, when the location is so unavailable as Eastern Europe is to American cyclists, but it would be an act of injustice to Roumania were we not to admit it the most beautiful of countries, and the northern section the most perfect of cycling routes. Where the valleys narrow into a pass, the road, cut into the side of rocks, is shaded by overhanging cliffs, and at short intervals are situated moss-covered wooden troughs, through which trickle ice water, clear as only snow water can be when percolated through porous rock. We were rudely disturbed in our survey of entrancing scenery one bright morning by a soldier standing guard at a small house by the roadside. We were at Predeal, the border line between Roumania and Austria-Hungary. Mr. Boxshall, the American vice-consul at Bucharest, had given us letters from the Austro-Hungarian consul at Bucharest, and this, with my muchly-indorsed passport, made an important looking package document which I had handed two officers in the examining room of the outpost. After a careful perusal of the papers, they respectfully declined to inspect our luggage and permitted us to pass into Hungary territory. Tomasu, an Austro-Hungarian customs house, was five miles north, and as we did not expect further formality until reaching that point, we set out at a lively pace as soon as our papers had been returned. We had proceeded scarcely a hundred yards ere a trooper in uniform stepped from a sentry-box and commanded us to halt. As he possessed a rifle and a business-like expression, we checked up immediately. An officer now appeared and demanded receipts for sixty florins, which should have been paid on our bicycles as revenue bond. The sixty florins, he explained, would be returned to us on our departure from Austrian territory, but as our entire finances did not greatly exceed that sum, we endeavored to appease the demands of the revenue department by a display of papers. The official after questioning us regarding our trip, became gracious, and returning our papers, motioned us to go ahead without further annoyance. Having successfully run the gauntlet on two occasions, the task at Tomasu was comparatively easy—in fact a pleasure—the officials endorsing our papers, inviting us to luncheon and providing us with maps. Leaving Tomasu, the grade was in our favor, and late in the afternoon we halted at the village inn at Persani. Stepping inside to quench our thirst, two men who had taken an unusual interest in our bicycles and selves drew near to listen to our conversation. One chap had an enormous revolver, and as the other stood with feet far apart, he thrust his hands under the tails of his smock. There was something familiar in the attitude, and I could not but exclaim to my wife, "I will bet a hundred dollars that chap has hip pockets in his trousers, and if he has, he has been in America." The word America settled all doubt. The pair advanced and declared themselves. In typical "contract labor" dialect. I was addressed as "Boss," informed that America was "bully," and that they had "built" a railroad at Salem, Ohio, and had brought home hip pockets filled with big guns and American money. They insisted upon buying us beer in true American style, and as they departed with a low bow, they looked at the common herd of untraveled with haughty air.

We endured slight showers during the afternoon of June 29, which proved our undoing for a century run. After a hard fall on one of the slippery hills, I limped into Peterfalva, 85 miles away from our starting point at midnight, the front fork of my wheel badly bent, and the grips broken from the handle-bars. A half-drunken blacksmith, whom I found in the village the next morning, made an aggravating botch of the repair, but it lasted to Muhlenbach, eighteen miles distant, where a cyclist kindly escorted me to a repair shop. The foreman of the shop had read of the Inter Ocean tourists, and promised us a permanent repair. He kept his word, and we again started on our journey at 6 in the evening. Twenty miles out of Muhlenbach a storm broke upon us and for two hours no cyclists ever had such hard riding, unless, of course, it be up the snow-clad mountains of Persia. We eventually found a wine house on the roadside, to which we were admitted, but informed that we could not be permitted to pass the night there. We flatly refused to go, and when the fat wife of the proprietor realized that we meant just what we said, she brought in straw and arranged a bed for us, where we slept until daylight. At Broos, where we stopped for breakfast, a jolly young fellow introduced himself to us as Erlich Janos, captain of the local wheel club, a pilot of Thomas Stevens, American World's cyclist of '85, and an admirer of the Inter Ocean tourists. Erlich Janos, or, as we should call him, John Erlich, had maps of a territory through which we would travel, and he asked permission to accompany us on part of the run. We were delighted to have him, and our admiration for him was doubled when he appeared in modern wheeling costume in the seat of one of the latest made machines. We covered thirty miles before halting for luncheon, and the good-natured cyclist continued with us as far as a fork in the road ten miles from Dobra. July 4 was spent on a lovely stretch of road, whirling toward Buda-Pesth. Heavy rains made the road almost impassable on July 5, but we foolishly attempted to press on and reach Kecskemet by 10 o'clock that night. When about eighteen miles from our destination, I was blinded by a flash of lightning, and the next moment pitched over a steep embankment. My damaged front fork was once more broken, and my leg seriously wrenched. The situation was anything but pleasant, and how we ever reached Kecskemet carrying the broken wheel and feeling our way in the darkness, remains this day a source of wonder to ourselves. We arrived in the city just in time to catch the mail train into Buda-Pesth, fifty-one miles north, where our wheels were repaired and our broken journey once more picked up.

Though our arrival in the city was unannounced and detracted from by entrance on the conventional railway, the Buda-Pesth cyclists immediately accepted us as wandering members of a vast fraternity. Mr. Emil Philopivich, Mr. Otto Blathy and Mr. Joseph Erlich were active in our behalf, and if we do not know the principal sights of the Hungarian capital, the error is not with them. When we left Buda-Pesth on July 17, with Messrs. Erlich and Philopivich as pace-makers, we had in trail many cyclists journeying from Buda-Pesth to Vienna. Assisted by smooth roads, we were in a fair way of reaching Vienna by night, but a cold rain sent us scurrying into a hotel on the roadside, delaying us until the next morning. We reached the outskirts of Vienna at 10 o'clock in the morning, wheeling into the city through scores of parks, avenues of beautiful buildings, and squares reserved for the erection of some government structure designed to match some magnificent building already rearing its proud dome on the square opposite. Vienna would be a paradise to cyclists if the street pavements and condition of thoroughfares were not a menace to life and limb. There is not a street but that has suffered severe attacks of gas, water and sewage contraction. The result is a maze of holes, ditches, depressions and bumps. There are many places to visit in Vienna and near by, but one of the first runs we made was far out in the suburbs to a cottage occupied by a Mr. Clemens. Few people in the book-reading world know Mr. Clemens, but millions know Mark Twain, and the pair are as closely united as Dr. Jekyl and Mr. Hyde (yet in justice to Mr. Clemens, not so dissimilar in character). Mr. Clemens was situated in a delightful, quiet spot, hard at work, while his daughters were adding to their musical education the desired Viennese polish. I did not ascertain what fountain-pen he used, get a diagram of the house with a cross representing where he sat at work, or even his signature asserting that I had a genuine interview with him, but I know that he was enjoying good health, was vigorous as ever, smoked good cigars, and said we were welcome.

We liked Vienna and its people, and we stayed in the city just long enough to enjoy its pleasures and learn only a few of its inconveniences. The Inter Ocean cyclists had decided to depart westward July 27, and the "Neue Wiener Tagblatt," which had announced every movement we had made, did not lose advantage of a final write-up. Early in the morning of the date agreed upon we were aroused by a visitor. He was a cyclist and came to announce that hundreds of people were awaiting us in the Kohlmarkt, and though the hour was 7 o'clock and we were to start at 9, the people would be pleased if we would remain on exhibition during the interval. The idea did not suit us exactly, and communicating the fact to the delegate through closed doors, we again slept the sleep of people who must do two days' work in one. We reached the Kohlmarkt at 9 o'clock, and, as our early informant had stated; a crowd awaited us. It was a Vienna crowd, good-natured and patient, who cheered us as we wheeled into sight, made way for us to pass to the rendezvous, but almost pulled us to pieces in efforts to shake hands with us and attract attention to their hearty "Gleich lich ze reisen."

We pulled out into the street at 9:30 o'clock. Our escort and the police held back the crowd long enough to allow a photographer to add two negatives to his collection, and then with a sigh of relief we slipped into our saddles and wheeled slowly through the lane of shouting people. Our escort was a unique one, the riders clad in white flannel, black hose, and lavender silk sweaters. Mr. Charles Carpenter, Miss Marion Carpenter and Mr. Fritz of Pottstown, Pa., also lined up, and with a constantly accumulating line of cyclists we started toward the western limits. Near St. Poiten we had lunch, our companions returned to Vienna, and the Inter Ocean cyclists wheeled on alone. We halted that night sixty-four miles from where we had left our Vienna party at midday. We were again in the realm of gast-houses, plain but substantial meals, odd little chambers, equipped with two bedsteads, one chair, a washstand, and several feather beds. It is pleasant, though, clean, and our only regret at the resumption of our trip was that we had left behind Vienna, a city which cannot be excelled in gayety, life and beauty. Paris may be more wicked, vicious and historical in strife, but there is only one Vienna, and that a peerless city of beauty and wholesome pleasure.

Lector House believes that a society develops through a two-fold approach of continuous learning and adaptation, which is derived from the study of classic literary works spread across the historic timeline of literature records. Therefore, we aim at reviving, repairing and redeveloping all those inaccessible or damaged but historically as well as culturally important literature across subjects so that the future generations may have an opportunity to study and learn from past works to embark upon a journey of creating a better future.

This book is a result of an effort made by Lector House towards making a contribution to the preservation and repair of original ancient works which might hold historical significance to the approach of continuous learning across subjects.

HAPPY READING & LEARNING!

LECTOR HOUSE LLP
E-MAIL: lectorpublishing@gmail.com

www.ingramcontent.com/pod-product-compliance
Lightning Source LLC
Chambersburg PA
CBHW020728160726
47993CB00006B/2378